Going **FARTHER**

EXPERIENCE THE POWER AND LOVE OF
GOD THAT TURNS TRAGEDY INTO TRIUMPH

VAHEN KING

Kat,
He sees your tears and
he will comfort
you.
Vahen

# Endorsements

"Vahen hopes to one day be a missionary in Africa" was the introduction given at her high school graduation. Pursuing that dream, Vahen graduated Bible College and was living life to the fullest, engaged to be married to the *"love of her life."* Then tragedy! She was unprepared for the roller coaster ride life had in store for her. Diagnosed with Transverse Myelitis which resulted in paralysis and bowel and bladder control issues, her life spiraled out of control.

The core of ministry is in acknowledging that God has given each of us a story and being willing to share that story of how we have seen God's faithfulness in our lives.

Join with Vahen in her story as she experiences helplessness and hopelessness and goes from independence to interdependence. You will laugh, cry, hope, and pray with her as she meticulously weaves the story of God's love and grace into the fabric of her life. Get ready to vicariously join her and experience the power and love of God that turns a litany of tragedies into miraculous triumph! Vahen's story will inspire you to trust God and triumph! In *Going Farther,* she goes deeper with God, and, yes, eventually, to Africa!

Pastor Clarence Buckle
General Secretary-Treasurer
Pentecostal Assemblies of Newfoundland & Labrador

Vahen King is a strong, passionate woman of God with a heart to share the love of Christ with a world of hurting people. Her book *Going Farther* provides the reader with an intimate reflection of the struggles she has faced in her life and the amazing tenacity that she has found not only to cope with them, but to victoriously overcome them! Vahen's life is a living testament of Romans 8:28 which states "And we know that God causes all things to work together for good to those who love God, to those who are called according to His purpose." (NASB) I invite you to journey along with my dear friend through the pages of her personal life story and discover that in life our greatest blessings are not always found in simply reaching our destination but in the miracles that we encounter along the way.

Tammy Richards
Registered Nurse and Friend
Occupational Health Manager, Covenant Health
Edmonton, Alberta

———————————— ∞ ————————————

Going Farther is the powerful story of one woman's journey to be all that God has designed her to be. While the circumstances and challenges may be different, it is truly my story – and it is your story. Vahen King opens our eyes to living that requires a continual deepening trust in God, a divinely provided determination to not give up, and reliance on Holy Spirit to do what we cannot accomplish. This book is not the end of her story but it provides a foundation that we all need to go farther with God than we or others could ever expect.

Rev. David Hall
Director for Leader Development & Care
Pentecostal Assemblies of Alberta & Northwest Territories District
Edmonton, Alberta

———————————— ∞ ————————————

This book is more than a story of personal struggle to overcoming adversity. It is an intricately woven narrative handcrafted by God to impact countless others for His kingdom. Vahen King, once the 'unlikely' writer, was from the beginning hand-picked by God to share her life on a public stage. Like the tenacity she brings to her workouts, she has an even greater fire for her ministry. There is no mask that could hide her love for God, her personal relationship with Jesus Christ, and her desire to serve Him.

Nancy Morrow
Kinesiologist/Exercise Therapist/Vahen's Personal Trainer
Edmonton, Alberta

Darkness can be scary. Uncertainty, fear, and anxiety can easily grip any heart. *Going Farther* is a reminder that when we journey through the darkest times of our lives, God is with us. Vahen's story is an inspiration for those of you who are traveling through your own season of darkness. It reminds us that there is a God who walks with us and holds us up when we are not able to do so on our own. *Going Farther* will inspire you to pursue the heart of God. Enjoy this inspirational read.

Mike Freake
Pastor, Host and Executive Producer of Heart Matters
and high school friend to Vahen King
Gander, Newfoundland and Labrador
www.evangelgander.ca
www.Heartmatters.tv

Get ready to move forward in your own journey with the Lord as you join Vahen King in her story. You will marvel at the many amazing ways the Lord spoke prophetically to Vahen as He confirmed His purposes in her life. The journey will be a candid exposure of some of the popular lies that the Lord graciously dismantled as He restored her dreams.

It was over 15 years ago that I first met Vahen. I remember first seeing her seated in the service in her wheelchair. Her radiant smile and the warmth of her heart really didn't "fit" with that chair! The story was just being scripted at that point. She has courageously pushed past both pitfalls and shallow finish lines. As you read, the words "walk by faith" will take on new meaning. You will have a fresh view for your own life as you journey in these pages with her to horizons of hope—authentic hope. *Going Farther* will take you into the discovery of how disability became dependency on her never-failing God!

Rev. Peggy I. Kennedy
Two Silver Trumpets Ministries
Speaker & Author
Beamsville, Ontario

Vahen's book will take you on a journey through a life filled with love, laughter, God, and family, but also a life filled with pain, sadness, and unbelievable challenges! Her story will leave you feeling inspired and awestruck by the woman behind it.

I have known Vahen for many years and have always felt amazed by what she does and how she does it. The challenges life has presented for Vahen have been met and conquered time and time again by this beautiful and strong person.

Holly Mascioli
B.A.B.F (Bachelor of Applied Business in Finance) and Friend
Edmonton, Alberta

As you read the first few words of this marvelous true story, you will be compelled to "go farther" until you've finished the book.

Vahen, a dear friend of mine, has lived every aspect of this narrative and continues to inspire me every occasion I meet with her. I highly recommend you soak up every turn in her life's journey, learn from her every lesson, and move forward in your own life.

She is a living example of what God does in a life that is committed to His design and purposes. This account will make you laugh, cry, be inspired, ask questions, and encourage you to "walk with God farther" than you could think possible.

Rev. Larry Lindoff
B.Ed., Dip. Theo., M.Div., D. Min [Studies]
Pastoral Care at Evangel Pentecostal Assembly
www.evangel.info/_ministries/_pastoralcare
Edmonton, Alberta

Table of Contents

Joy In the Morning

I know there's joy in the morning.
I don't think I can wait until then.
Fear comes, without any warning.
I find myself searching again.
I could try to stop the tears from falling,
but I'm not one to pretend.
So please come and meet me, where I am.
Come and, meet me where I am.
I don't know how I could walk to you,
when I can hardly stand.
Joy in the morning.

Kelly Marie Elford
Download her song for free at: https://soundcloud.com/kellyelford
kellyelfordmusic@outlook.com
All songs written and performed by Kelly Elford ©

Dedication

This book is dedicated to anyone who has ever had to walk through personal struggles or overcome adversity. God planted in me the desire to write this book to those who have felt fearful, unworthy, or unloved. I have learned much about *undeserved* love, forgiveness, and the power to overcome. And, I am so thankful that I have *not* received what I *deserved.*

Some who read this may be able to relate on some level with my story, but others may want to cry out, "That's great for you; but, you don't know *my* story."

I want you to know that no matter where you are or where you have been, God *is* enough! That's what matters. My heart's desire is that you will also experience the power and freedom that comes from a life of intimacy with Christ.

I believe that even now the Lord is restoring hope to those who call upon Him. He is a God who wants to give more than we could ever hope or dream. This book, *Going Farther,* is dedicated to you. May you know you *are* forgiven! May you know you *are* worthy! And may you know you *are* loved!

Foreword

I have never known Vahen except in a wheelchair. When we finally met, her chair was already an established fact. There are many times in our conversations when the idea of "when I can walk again" comes up. Somewhere deep inside me my horrified response is "But I can't keep up with you now! What would it be like if you didn't have that chair to slow you down?" She's a "blue streak!" I still vividly remember the occasion when her husband Vaughan had traveled ahead across the country to find a new job and new home with the promise to be back in a month to collect "Blue." Halfway through that month she decided that loneliness and separation were not her thing, so she trundled her suitcase and wheelchair into her car and drove for FIVE DAYS to be reunited. That was one incident of many that spells out the determination and perseverance of this spirited daughter-in-law.

Since the beginning of writing this book, "Blue" has sent me snapshots to read and provide my input. One day when all the unedited chapters arrived, I remember my feelings of frustration that I didn't have time in the foreseeable future to read them. But late that evening the cursor went directly to them. I couldn't stop until I'd read the whole book. It's been a long time since I've read a book that made me so emotionally involved. I saw her heart. (I also admit I was pretty pumped with the author!)

The testimony of her book *Going Farther* is dead on. She brings up key points that move this story from just biography to quiet and solid exhortation. Her wholeness, authority, and anointing to impact people will be utilized as she illustrates being with God first. The practical experiences that Vahen shares in

Going Farther are already enabling her to be His world changer.

John King
International Bible Teacher
Father-in-law, aka "Father John"

――――――――――――― ∽ ―――――――――――――

My life was changed when I met Vahen. I knew we were a perfect match and it wasn't only because our names were so similar! We both shared many common interests and beliefs—one of which was in the deep friendship and fellowship of a personal God.

I don't think my situation is all that extra-ordinary. Bad things happen to everyone—everyone has a story. Before I was married to Vahen, a co-worker took me aside and told me there is no shame in backing out of my wedding plans since my situation had changed. Their advice was that I re-evaluate my commitment to this girl. Although their concern was with good intentions, I couldn't accept their perspective that my life would be over if I married this girl in a wheelchair. People say that I have such a great testimony because I was willing to make a difficult decision and stick by a person who just had her world pulled out from under her. But, how could I do otherwise? Even though I didn't know why something like this would happen to Vahen, I believe God is in control of everything and Vahen was still the same girl I fell in love with.

When Vahen first came to me and told me she was writing her story, I asked her, "Are you sure? What do we have to share? We're not perfect or have everything figured out. We've struggled financially, spiritually and emotionally. Do we really need to tell the world about our life, our mistakes, and our challenges?" I didn't want to be in the centre of attention, but I accepted that God gave her a desire to write her story and that it could be a way for her to inspire and minister to others as well. Over the last 3 years I've never seen anyone more dedicated or determined to complete this enormous task. When I finally read her first draft earlier this year, it dug up a lot of forgotten emotions and memories. With tears in my eyes, I had to thank Vahen for being a part of *my* life, especially through some of these challenging times. We both had to take responsibility for our mistakes and for opportunities missed. I guess that is what makes relationships so real!

Life is defined by our experiences and, while no one enjoys a bad experience, they happen to all of us. In this book Vahen shares how she was able to overcome these struggles and change her life story into one of joy and encouragement. I'm proud of Vahen's determination and accomplishments. She is an inspiration even to me. I invite you now to share in a story that is still being written by the One who loves unconditionally. He is our God and we've chosen to put our trust in Him.

Vaughan King
Vahen's husband and best friend

♡*Introduction*

For the longest time I doubted myself and my abilities. I felt I just couldn't move forward. I always knew I wanted to do more or be more, but my search to know the cause of what was limiting me took a while. Finally, I realized that the only thing holding me back was my fear! But what was I afraid of? Fear of failure? Fear of people's opinions of me?

As I continued to search for that root cause of what was constantly limiting me, the question never left me: "What am I afraid of?" In my heart I knew that I would find the answer. Many times I had been asked, "How do you do it?" "How do you get the strength to keep going?" "Do you not have any fear?" My response would always be, "Of course I still have fear, but my relationship with God helps me go farther. It gives me the strength to "push past" what it "feels like" and not let fear hold me back." I think Bruce H. Wilkinson said it best when he said, "People often feel that because they are afraid of something, they do not have the courage to conquer it. However, courage is not the absence of fear: rather it's choosing to act in spite of fear[1]."

At the beginning of 2015, I felt that this year would be the year of pushing past even more of my fears. I had entered the season of "being more." As I began embracing this, the results have become more than I ever expected.

I have been in a wheelchair since 1999 due to a medical condition called Transverse Myelitis. Now, after 17 years, I have just taken my first steps unassisted! My dreams of doing and being more are becoming more of a reality than I ever thought

---

1 Bruce Wilkinson, *The Dream Giver*: Following your God-Given Destiny (Multnomah Books, 2003), p.93

possible. I have had people ask me when I was going to publish my story. My response was to laugh at their suggestion and tell them, "I'm not a writer." But now, after about three years of hard work and determination, I've published my first book. I have had to relive some deeply personal and painful times, as well as some of the best highlights of my life. However, through all the highs and lows, I am thrilled to share my journey with the world around me.

I have learned from my own experience that you don't actually have the power to control your life. The sudden onslaught of a paralyzing medical condition was a major contradiction to my "own power." In my recovery process there definitely was a role I had to play. However, as I rediscovered my relationship with God, He showed me that I can only go so far in my own strength. With Him I could go farther than I ever hoped or imagined if I let go of my fear. Every day I had to make tough choices, and the way I responded to my choices determined whether or not I could go farther. My new perspective allows me to look ahead with great expectation. I am thankful to God for all my happiness and success. It is because of Him I am facing my fears and going farther. Thank you for taking this journey with me. I have chosen to put my name in Philippians 1:6 "...being confident of this very thing, that He who has begun a good work in me will complete it until the day of Jesus Christ."

♡Chapter 1

The Little Redhead

It appeared as though I was always destined to stand out and be different. Even in my childhood it seemed I was being defined by my red hair, freckles, and a personality to match! That continued into my college days as I was known as a social butterfly. Later, even in the rehab hospital surrounded by my own pain and the pain of others, I was nicknamed "Smiles."

All the way through my childhood I was a little girl who spoke her mind and always seemed to attract attention--good or bad! It was all the same in my young mind. When I was in grade one there was an outbreak of head lice at my school. Being only five years old, I didn't understand that this wasn't something a person would want. The nurse called my mother to inform her that I was infected. She told her she had to come get me immediately. Much to everyone's dismay, I had already joined my friends on the bus for the ride home by the time my mother arrived. When I saw her I stood to my feet with my arm stretched high in the air and my little fingers wrapped tightly around the bottle the nurse gave me. I yelled out to her with excitement: "Mom! Mom! I've got the crawlers!" I was so thrilled to have been singled out for something.

In my family we knew that God was a strong part of what gave life meaning. Family prayer time and going to church at least three times per week may have become a "ritual," but I did develop a strong sense of who God was. A relationship with God meant that He loved me unconditionally. I always tried hard to do the "right thing." If at times I did the "wrong thing," I would ask forgiveness and I knew He would forgive me. I asked Jesus into my heart when I was five years old. I knew I wanted to serve God and do something great for Him. This was not because I thought I was anything special, but because I always felt a strong desire to seek what God wanted.

There was an intern pastor at our church when I was about 7 years old. By this time, I had quite a clear realization of who God was. Listening to this man teach us was very exciting because he would always get the children involved. I especially liked it when he asked for volunteers. I vividly recall one time when I was chosen to come to the front for the next "illustration." He said, "I have a choice for you. In my one hand I have a crisp, new five-dollar bill. In my other hand I have a Bible. You can have whichever one you want."

My first thought was, "How cool it would be to have the money!" Five dollars was a lot for a five-year-old. However, I made my decision: "I choose the Bible, please." He replied, "Okay, you can have the Bible." Before giving me my prize, he opened the Bible to reveal another crisp five-dollar bill tucked in the pages. My little eyes grew wide and I asked in awe, "Can I really have both?" "Yes, you can have both," he said. Then he read the scripture verse that he had written on the inside,

"But seek first the kingdom of God and His righteousness, and all these things shall be added to you." Matthew 6:33 At that time I don't think I truly understood the weight of that lesson. However, the Lord was depositing a very important principle in my heart: "If I trust Him, I can have both."

As a teenager I never really saw myself as someone who wanted to be a doctor or a lawyer. I just knew that I had a heart of compassion and I wanted to make a positive impact on the world. Beyond a shadow of a doubt, I knew that was my calling. As I walked across the stage to receive my diploma at my high school graduation my life's goal was announced: "Vahen hopes to one day be a missionary in Africa."

For this little redhead, the journey ahead was going to be far from a straight line to those lofty plans. The unexpected was waiting for me just around the corner. With all these big dreams and aspirations to do great things for God, how was it possible that my world would get so drastically turned upside down? How could I go from being that little girl whose only desire was to love and serve God to someone who not only resented God but also doubted His existence? Within a few years after that promise-filled announcement at high school graduation my life would be spiraling out of control. I would stop feeling or caring about anyone around me and my marriage would be on the verge of collapse. My teenage dream of being a missionary or making a positive impact on the world didn't even matter anymore. Instead, I would be struggling to cope with the reality of a meaningless life of brokenness and pain from this wheelchair.

Allow me to share with you how God has turned my pain into this beautiful platform of peace I now enjoy. In the past when I would read James 1:2-3, I would even become angry with God: "…count it all joy when you fall into various trials, knowing that the testing of your faith produces patience." However, now as I look back at my pain and my struggles, I can say,

"Thank you, God." I even tell others that I feel I have this unfair advantage in life. People think it's so amazing that as a person with a disability, I have been able to do things like downhill skiing, rock climbing, or zip lining to name a few. However, the funniest thing is that I get the same reaction when people find out that I drive or that I shop for my own groceries. I get praised for doing the normal every-day task. That sounds like an unfair advantage to me!

I am not professing to have all the answers or even say I understand what you may be going through. And yes, I still have my struggles. But, as I share my journey with you, I would like the opportunity to show you how God turned my life of pain and anger into something more beautiful than I could ever imagine. I am an overcomer!

♡Chapter 2

My Will vs. Surrender

I was in grade eleven when my dad became the pastor of a small church in Gambo, Newfoundland and Labrador[2]. I remember the pain of leaving my friends behind and moving to a town where I knew no one. Yes, I was a social butterfly and loved meeting new people, but this was a lot to cope with. My dad was making the change from being a fisherman to being a "fisher of men." I knew this was the right thing for our family, but I also knew it would not be easy.

It was a little church in the middle of town. Our house was attached to the side of the church building. There was a door and a small hallway connecting our house to the front entrance of the church. I actually remember one time my mom walked out into the prayer meeting and forgot she was still wearing her slippers!

From that first Sunday, I was faced with the reality of the monumental task set before us. My dad and I were at the front. Seated before us were my mom, my little sister, and two

---

2 An amendment to the Constitution officially changed the name of Newfoundland to Newfoundland and Labrador on December 6, 2001. The official abbreviations are: Newfoundland Nfld. Newfoundland and Labrador N.L. I will use the common name of "Newfoundland" throughout the remainder of the book as islanders tend to do. https://www.collectionscanada.gc.ca/obj/040006/f2/040006-02-e.pdf

other people. We made up the entire congregation!

Our church didn't have any musicians or singers. Since I had just learned to play an instrument called the Omnichord, I was the best and only candidate. I was very involved in most aspects of the church activities. This included nearly everything from assisting with the music for each service to helping with the kids' clubs.

I must admit that on many occasions I felt I was just going through the motions. I even asked God more than once, "Why can't I be a normal teenager and not have all this responsibility?" I wanted to fit in. Why couldn't I go dancing and drinking if I wanted like my other friends could? I guess I didn't really understand what it meant to truly surrender my will to God. I was struggling with the fact that although I still had a strong desire to follow God, I wanted some of the things of this world, too.

After graduating from high school, I decided to take a year off to figure out what I wanted to do. I knew I had a heart for God and I wanted to do something for Him, but I really didn't know what that looked like. During my year of soul-searching I lived with my parents, found a job nearby, and continued to be involved in our church.

We had some friends in a neighboring community who were also pastors of a local church. They requested a special speaker to come to one of their services. I was invited to sing. I chose a classic song called "I'd Rather Have Jesus[3]." The challenging first line is "I'd rather have Jesus than silver or gold." That night I sang most of the song through my tears. As always, whenever I sang that song, the part that always came alive in my heart

---

3 "I'd rather have Jesus than Silver or Gold." Hymn Writer: Rhea Miller, Music written by: George Beverly Shea; "Hymn History"; http://hishymnhistory.blogspot.ca/2012/11/id-rather-have-jesus.html

was, "I'd rather have Jesus than man's applause, I'd rather be faithful to His dear cause." I always felt such compassion when I sang these songs that were rich with words of surrender to God, but what did that mean? At times I felt my walk with God was just "routine;" yet, at other times I felt like I could almost touch heaven. As I sat in the back of the church that evening after I finished singing, my heart was so open as I heard the guest speaker talking about serving God and being in ministry.

After he spoke, he looked around and said, "There is someone here who God is calling to step out into full-time ministry." Those words tugged on my heart, and I looked around to see if anyone else was affected by his words like I was. He continued to say, "If you would come and see me, I would love to pray for God's protection and blessing on your life and ministry." I knew in my heart he was talking about me. With tears rolling down my face, I stepped out and walked down the aisle to meet the guest speaker. Before he finished praying for me he said, "Vahen, God strongly laid you on my heart while you were singing. He showed me your heart of compassion and that He has a special plan for your life."

During this year of soul-searching, I felt God was directing me toward full-time ministry. Even though I didn't really know how that would happen, I thought going to Bible College would be the next best step to bring me closer to the plan God had for me. After all, that's where people went when they wanted to equip themselves for ministry, right? So I applied to Eastern Pentecostal Bible College in Peterborough, Ontario. I thought "This is easy: I'll go to Bible College, get my degree, marry a pastor, and we'll share a life of ministry together. Praise God!" (Maybe I was a little naive?)

As my departure date approached, I became apprehensive about leaving home and my comfortable surroundings to travel thousands of miles away for an uncertain future in Ontario. I was having more and more doubts. Was this the right choice? Was God really calling me? Although this was a scary step of faith, I really did have a calm assurance that I was moving toward my future.

My parents decided to drive me to my campus. They turned this trip into a fun family vacation. However, I knew my parents were probably just wanting to hang on to me as long as possible. This was a big move for a sheltered newfie girl, and they knew I would need all the support I could get.

Since we were from a small town in Newfoundland and had never left the province before, this was definitely going to be the best trip ever. We even found driving the thousands of miles an adventure. We enjoyed every minute of the trip. As we neared our destination, my sister Erica and I asked to go to Canada's Wonderland which is a special theme park in Ontario. I also saw this as an added bonus because it provided me with a much needed distraction. When mom and dad agreed, the excitement could not be contained, and our anticipation built during the 3-day drive to Ontario. Finally, after all the driving, we arrived. This was a big deal.

Even today my sister and I talk about some of our memories at Canada's Wonderland. Everything was so new for us and we enjoyed everything including the long line ups for tickets and food and, of course, the wild rides.

I admit that my sister was the most adventurous of our family. She wanted to go on all the rides. I just wanted to enjoy the huge water slides and float down the lazy river in the water park. I didn't have the nerve to go on any big rides. The thought of roller coasters made me sick--literally! I was so glad when my dad agreed to be the brave one and offered to go on those rides with her. We were surprised when they returned from the rides much sooner than we expected. Erica explained, "We were in line for a roller coaster. As we watched the line getting shorter and shorter, I saw Dad's face was growing more pale. I realized that I didn't have the heart to make him do this."

Our dad was always there for us. He would give us the car with a full tank of gas, have our breakfast ready almost every morning before school, or even drive us to school when we were literally only 3 minutes away. "It's raining" or "I'm running late" were our regular excuses. I'm sure in that roller coaster line up when my sister turned to him and said, "Dad, we don't have to do this," he felt relieved. She knew he'd do it if he had to, but I'm sure he was really happy that he didn't have to.

I can honestly say, this trip was one of the best family vacations ever. When my family drove me to the Bible College campus and moved me into my dorm room a lot of reality set in. Many emotions filled my heart as they pulled away. A new chapter had begun.

Shortly after my parents left, I was sitting and talking with a really good friend of mine from home whose parents were the pastors from that neighboring community I mentioned before. It was great that she was going to be here at Bible College with me, but I was feeling afraid and wasn't sure how I was going to be strong and face my unknown future. During our conversation before her father left, something he said to me struck my heart. "Vahen, in your walk with God and in your future ministry, there will be many moments when you will feel stretched like an elastic band. When you think you can't stretch any more, God will take you farther. Stay close to Him and He will sustain you. You will grow stronger in Him; He will not let you break." Little did I know how powerfully that message would play out in my life!

♡Chapter 3

Did I Lose My Dream?

My first Bible College semester started and it wasn't long before classes were in full swing. It was quite the experience for this sheltered girl from a small town in Newfoundland. This was no longer a fun retreat but rather a grueling semester of theology, doctrines, and new perspectives. It was pretty overwhelming at first. After I found out we were expected to manage our own time and marks, it didn't seem so bad. I spent a lot of time playing school sports and enjoyed being a social butterfly around campus.

One day in my first-year theology class, the professor expressed a view that I didn't believe to be true. Without thinking it through, I passionately spoke my mind and stormed out of the class. How could I have known the door would slam so loudly? Before the door closed, I heard my professor say, "I will see you in my office later."

Uncertain as to how this meeting would go, I knocked on his office door and quietly entered. The conversation started out much differently than I had imagined. "Welcome!" he said, in a chipper voice. "It's so refreshing to see a young lady standing up and being confident in herself." After getting over the shock of not having to fight for my beliefs, I let out a sigh of relief. I then had a chance to share my heart and express how I felt about the topic discussed earlier. I don't really remember much more about the conversation other than it was a pleasant one. Rumor had it that from that day on I was the professor's pet. Apparently, he was impressed by people who stand up for themselves instead of being weak and timid and always telling him only what they thought he wanted to hear!

It appeared that although I had started off on the right foot by standing up for what I believed, there seemed to always be "something" that tested my faith or beliefs and made me question God. Looking back, I realize that these "tests" were really growing my knowledge and faith. I remembered the scripture in James 1:3 that said, "...count it all joy when you fall into various trials, knowing that the testing of your faith produces patience." Of course, it never feels like it's a good thing when you are going through it.

Throughout the school year we all attended the weekly chapel in the gymnasium. On one particular chapel day they held a prayer line. Anyone who wanted prayer could go forward and the staff would pray for them. When I got to the front of the line the president of the college prayed over me. "God, I pray for Vahen. I pray that you will bless her ministry. I also pray that you will bless her body from her head to her feet, right down to her digestive system. Dear God, protect her in her ministry." I thought, "That's an interesting and descriptive prayer although a bit unusual. It's okay, God, I'll take all the prayer I can get."

Even though Bible College was a struggle for me I was feeling great. I knew I was where God wanted me to be. I was going to get my degree and enter a world He was leading me to. I was filled with so much hope. Unfortunately, my love for sports and socializing had caused me to fall behind with my academics in my first year. As a result, I was constantly struggling to catch up. Worse still, I wasn't allowed to play on the college volleyball team again until I managed to bring my grades up.

In order to improve my grades in my second year, I decided to get a tutor. That decision turned out even better than I expected. Yes, my tutor did help me with my grades, but he also stole my heart. We had a beautiful relationship that I knew would end with an "I do." I had an extra incentive to work hard to impress. Although it was really hard for this social butterfly, I took extra classes over the summer to get back on track and make a comeback in my third year.

As I began my fourth and final year, I didn't waste any time arranging a meeting with the college counselor to discuss my course load and graduation status. I was confident that I had succeeded in getting my grade point average up enough to play volleyball again. I was already feeling the excitement. However, the words I heard were not the words I was expecting. It was like pouring water on a fire and it actually made me sick to my stomach. I was told that, for whatever reason, I did not have the right courses to graduate with a four-year degree. To make matters worse, my grades were still not what I needed to be able to play college sports.

No! This wasn't what I had signed up for! I was then given a choice: stay another year and graduate with a full degree or graduate with my current class this year with a three-year diploma. All my hard work and extra hours seemed to be pointless. Even though my grades had improved since I had consistently worked with my tutor, they still weren't enough. I was so angry. I wanted to hop on the first plane home and just forget about going into the ministry.

I was feeling so let down and confused. I couldn't make sense of anything. After several long phone conversations with my parents and many tears, I prayed that God would give me a sign and let me know that I was still where He wanted me to be. I said "God, if you are still with me and I am still where you want me to be, let someone give me a candy today".

It's funny because I never usually get that specific with my requests to God, but for some reason this time I did. Without another thought of my crazy prayer, I went about my day. As I was getting ready for another class, my neighbor, who was also from Newfoundland, surprised me, "Vahen, I just got a package from home and wanted to know if you'd like to share some of these "newfie candies" with me?" Well, you can imagine how that made me feel. I quickly said, "Yes! Absolutely!" I got to share with her all about what I had just been through and how she was an answer to my "odd" prayer request.

I was so excited that God cared enough about me to reach me in spite of my weak faith. I said "Okay, God, I know you are with me, thank you. I've made it this far, I can't quit now." I decided to stay and try to keep my focus on God and the reason I came here in the first place. I decided whether it was a diploma or degree, God could still use me. After all, I was going to graduate with my soul mate and we would go into ministry together.

Each year I tried to spend Christmas with my family in Newfoundland. On my final year of Bible College I was even more excited than usual to be home for Christmas. My soon-to-be fiancé and I had been talking about our future and decided that since I might not get many more opportunities to shop for a wedding dress with my mom, I should take the opportunity to do it while home for the holidays. It was the best Christmas ever. I not only found the perfect dress but I also bought it for an amazing price.

Upon returning to college after Christmas I started looking

forward with great expectation to Valentine's Day. I was certain that getting an engagement ring was the next step. I was pretty confident it would happen soon, since we had gone ring browsing several months before.

Valentine's Day came and went with no ring or proposal, but I was still convinced that we were meant to be and that it would happen soon. In his attempt to help ease my disappointment, he told me that it was okay for me to work on our wedding invitations. Even though I wanted to run right out and get started, I said that we should wait until our engagement was official. Then one night, not long after that, he said to me, "Vahen, we need to talk." I thought, "Wow, this is the night!" I had this feeling many times before, but this time I was sure he was going to propose. I just wondered how he was going to do it. We had talked many times before about what we would do when we got married. We had even gone to interviews as a couple for potential positions in ministry. I was convinced that this was going to be the special night. I could not have been more wrong. Instead of a proposal, he said that he didn't know if there was a future for us and that we couldn't be together. I was stunned! What did he mean? This made no sense to me. How could this be? I thought that God had brought us together. How then can this be the end? How could I have been so wrong?

My world had crumbled around me yet again. I didn't know how I would be able to go on this time. I did not see how I would ever get through my pain. For the days and weeks that followed, my talks with God were more like me saying, "God, I know you will bring him back, but please help me endure this pain as I wait." With no answers to give me closure, I thought for sure it was a classic case of, "If you love something set it free; if it's meant to be it will come back." My heart was convinced he would come back because I didn't know how I could go on without him.

Feeling broken-hearted, angry, and alone, I was sure that God had abandoned me. Things were oh, so far out of control. I could not make any sense of this sudden and crushing turn of events. I doubted if I even had any capacity left to trust God. All I could seemingly hear was silence. I wondered where God was in all of this. It was a very devastating experience to endure. It would only be after many more years and after much more time getting to know God better that I could look back on that situation and realize that He had *not* abandoned me. Rather, He was directing my life in a way that I would be so thankful for. Even in what seemed like silence, He was speaking very loudly to me.

Still broken and feeling very hollow, I somehow managed to find the strength to stay and graduate. I ended my college days with much less passion and determination than when I started. Where would I fit into ministry now? What about all my dreams of doing great things for God and making an impact on the world? All my plans seem to have shattered and I was left feeling like I had no future. I still hoped I would find my passion for God and do something great for Him, but the reality of my situation kept me thinking, "Did I lose my dream?"

♡Chapter 4

One August Night

After graduating from Bible College in the spring of 1998, I felt confused and far from God. I had a void in my life that I was trying desperately to fill. I decided to stay in Peterborough, Ontario, and work full time. I was finding that each day blurred into the next. I went through the motions of work, eat, sleep, and repeat. I would cry myself to sleep and then wake up, pull myself together, and do it all over again. I didn't realize it at the time, but I think that was when I first started having strong feelings of resentment towards God. My life felt like a yo-yo. It seemed there was always one thing after another that I had to "get through" and trust God for. Always before I had somehow managed to find the strength to keep going, but this time was different. I just didn't seem to have it in me to keep going. I needed to find a way to numb this pain.

I didn't really feel like going to church anymore, so I started going out to the clubs. I loved to dance and soon embraced the drinking as a natural next step. This was a way I could dull the pain. I started down a path I knew was not pleasing to God. I pushed aside everything I knew to be true and started to look for fulfillment on my own. I knew in my heart that this would not bring me true happiness, but it was providing temporary relief. Many times I would leave work in Peterborough and drive straight to Toronto to meet up with a friend to go out to the clubs.

Looking for happiness in all the wrong places became my obsession. I tried to date this guy my friend knew, and I had no intention of 'resisting' temptations, if you know what I mean. He was not the "good guy" you would take home to your parents. Even my friend advised me against him, but I didn't care. I declared that I was done being a "good girl" and I wanted her to ask him if he would be interested in dating me. In my attempts to impress this guy, I actually tried smoking pot with him. It was awful! Apparently I inhaled way too much and actually had a hallucination. I was saying, "Where did everyone go? Why did you guys all leave me?" I truly thought everyone had left the room. What was I thinking? I knew that I was hurting and I was just trying anything to numb this pain and fill the void.

My attempt to impress a guy by smoking pot for the first time just didn't work. When my friend asked him what he thought of me, his response was that he just couldn't get involved because I was too good for him. What? No! I don't want to be good anymore! I didn't understand it because I felt far from "good." Deep in my heart I knew God was protecting me and that made me even more angry at God.

Then one summer night in early August, while I was out with some friends in Peterborough, I saw a guy that I had chatted with briefly at a convenience store almost a year earlier. Being the social butterfly I am, I decided to go over and say, "Hi."

At first there was some confusion on his face as he tried to place me. I reminded him about our previous brief conversation as we were waiting in line to pay for our purchases. I told him that I had been wearing a ball cap and buying a Halloween costume. After I refreshed his memory he blurted out, "Wow, you look amazing!" He might have been trying to say that I looked a lot different than the first time we met, but I enjoyed the compliment! We laughed about it and reintroduced ourselves. I thought, "Vaughan! What a sexy name." We continued talking for a while longer before I returned to be with my friends.

As I was leaving, Vaughan approached me and said, "Here, take my business card and call me sometime if you want." A couple days later I did go by his work to say, "Hello." I gave him my phone number. After a week of playing phone tag, we finally connected and talked for hours. However, in the middle of our phone call the battery in his cell phone died. When he called me back, he explained that his phone had died so he ran down to a convenience store beside his house to use the payphone. It was already after 10:00 p.m. at night, but he asked me if I wanted to go for a walk. I happily accepted the offer. We walked and talked for several more hours that evening. He was a real gentleman. He didn't even try to kiss me goodnight.

Before I met Vaughan, I had made the decision to return to Newfoundland to be around my family and friends. I had enrolled in a music school to take some piano and vocal training. I was scheduled to start in September. I felt I could not trust where my choices had been leading me and needed to be home to get my life back on track.

During our walk on that first relaxed evening I decided to be up-front about my plans for the fall. Even though I was flattered by Vaughan's attention, I told him I was only around for another three weeks. I felt it was only fair that he knew I would be leaving the province of Ontario for good. However, even though we both knew we had an undeniable connection, I was still angry at God and was not looking for any type of serious relationship. I had no desire to even think about trusting anyone this soon after my shattering loss.

I knew that even with as much as Vaughan and I had talked, he didn't know the real me. I felt inclined to share with him that I had just graduated from a Bible College and that my parents were pastors. I thought for sure he would run and not look back. I also told him that even though I was not where I wanted to be in my life right then, I really did have a heart to serve and follow God. I continued to explain that I didn't want to simply go to church, but I really wanted to be in ministry and make a difference.

Apparently what I thought would be the shocking deal-breaking information actually was the thing that drew him closer to me. He too was searching for deeper meaning in his life and had a heart for God. It turned out that his parents were missionaries and that he had grown up on the other side of the world on the mission field of Papua New Guinea. I could hardly believe my ears! This was the farthest thing from what I expected to hear! I was supposedly on the run and angry with God and I ran right into the son of missionary parents who himself had a heart for God! Only God could have arranged all of this.

I decided to use my remaining weeks as a distraction from my pain and just have fun. For the next three weeks Vaughan and I spent as much time as we could together. We went on many awesome dates. We would go rollerblading or take pictures on our walks in the park. We took picnics down by the lake to listen to the local music festivals and enjoyed the fireworks. We explored numerous scenic sights in the surrounding countryside in his red sports car.

Time passed by in a blur, but three weeks later my car was packed and I was ready to drive back home to Newfoundland. As great as this time together with Vaughan was, my heart was still in pieces. I was doubtful I would ever be able to trust it again. I was sure this was just a phase and it would just fall apart like everything else I had attempted. As we said our goodbyes, Vaughan told me that he would not accept that I was just going to walk out of his life after the amazing time we shared. He also joked about how closely our names matched. That was something else we had in common. (My name was Vahen Ings and his was Vaughan King.) Admittedly, this was probably not something you could build a future on, since anyone with a phone book could skip the whole dating thing, but he did have a point. It *was* pretty cool! He made me smile. Vaughan said he understood how I needed some space, but he wanted to put his name in right now to be the first guy in line for a chance at a relationship with me when I was ready.

This should have been a happy time in my life. I had just met an amazing guy who wanted to be with me. And, even though I soon arrived home to my caring family, I battled depression and anxiety. Weeks went by as I struggled with chest pain and sleepless nights. I didn't know what was real anymore. I knew something was missing, but I didn't know what to do to fix it. I also kept wondering what to do with my relationship with Vaughan.

I remembered a comment one of my professors made back in college: "Vahen, when you find your true love, you will blossom and open up like a rose." I actually did feel myself opening up but trusting was another thing. I was still remembering the betrayal from the early spring. Then one night, as I lay on my bed in tears, my father sat beside me and said, "Vahen, you have to let go and let Vaughan love you. Stop hanging on to the past and put your trust in God."

♡ *Chapter 5*

My Knight in Shining Armour

Somehow, with Vaughan being miles away, it was easier for me to consider developing a relationship with him. It allowed us to develop a friendship and to grow closer. Over these next few months we talked on the phone nearly every night and wrote letters back and forth. Our relationship was growing and we couldn't wait to see each other again. After school each day I'd run over to the library and wait in line to use the computer so I could send an email to Vaughan. (This was Newfoundland in the early years of the internet and dial-up access.)

Vaughan had been chipping away at my heart for three months. Confident that our connection was growing stronger because of our common dreams and interests, he decided to hop on a plane to visit me for my birthday. Unknown to me, he came with the intention of giving me a promise ring. After a couple days of getting to know my family, he asked my father if he could have his blessing to continue courting me and to eventually ask for my hand in marriage. My dad told Vaughan yes, he could continue to court me, but he also gave him some advice about me. He said, "When Vahen does something, she does it with 100% of her heart." Vaughan concluded that he was trying to tell him that when I decide to do something there is nothing that will hold me back. As my father, he advised Vaughan to be wise and willing to wait and yet be ready for when I made up my mind about him.

This whirlwind trip to Newfoundland became the opportunity to meet family and friends and to get to know each other better. It cemented the feeling that we were right for each other. At the end of our week together Vaughan surprised me with an elegant sapphire promise ring. He asked if I would be willing to wear it and look forward to sharing a future together. Oddly enough, despite all that I had been through and my depression and anxiety since returning home, I accepted both the ring and the promise of a different future without hesitation. I was thrilled!

Vaughan returned to Ontario and life was starting to look better. I truly believe that was a turning point in my emotional healing. From that moment, and with each conversation thereafter, I began opening up and trusting Vaughan even more. Our long distance romance went on for two more months. I found myself falling more and more in love with him. My renewed hope of a happy ending was like medicine to my broken heart.

One thing Vaughan told me when we were dating long-distance was that he usually would know within three months if a relationship was worth pursuing. He was looking for someone he could share the rest of his life with. He wouldn't stay in a relationship if he didn't see a future in it. I knew I had to return to Peterborough to see where this could go. I needed to follow my heart to know for sure if this was real.

Upon my return to Ontario, close friends of mine were very generous and provided accommodations for me while I looked for work. It's because of them I was able to return to Ontario as quickly as I did. It wasn't long before I had two part-time jobs. I was able to save enough money to buy a fairly new car to get back and forth to work and move into my own apartment. Over the next three months my relationship with Vaughan grew even stronger. We had no doubt but that we were perfect for each other.

Maybe this sounds like a crazy whirlwind romance that you only read about in books. However, we had so much in common and we complemented each other so well. Vaughan was the strong, logical type with a sensitive romantic side and I was a red-headed firecracker who was willing to take on the world. We both had a strong Christian background. My parents were pastors and I was raised in church. His parents were missionaries and he was raised across the ocean on the mission field. Actually I hadn't even had a chance to meet his parents yet because they had been working in New Zealand for the last 3 years and wouldn't be back for another few months.

After three months, I remembered Vaughan's comments about his relationship timeline and I started to wonder about our future. I was a little fearful and was wondering how he felt. Did he feel the same love that I felt? He still hadn't said those three words, but I wanted to scream them out. I was waiting for him to say it first! I teased him about his "three-month" rule and wanted to know if there was some reason why I should stick around or was there still a future for me here in Peterborough? He looked at me a little shyly and told me that he could definitely see a future with me here in Peterborough. I wonder if the conversation with my father flashed in his mind. It may be that even then those words were echoing in his heart: "When Vahen does something, she does it with 100% of her heart." What a standing reminder that he better be ready for when I made up mind about him.

It wasn't long after that until he said, "I love you" and all my fears just disappeared. Our love just kept growing. Our conversation soon included discussion of engagement rings. He tried to get my opinion on what size of diamond I wanted and when we should get engaged. He said, "Well, the bigger the diamond, the longer the wait to get engaged; but, if you want to get engaged sooner, then you will have to be happy with a smaller diamond." My thoughts were, "I've waited all my life for you and I want to marry you sooner rather than later."

On a Sunday afternoon on the long weekend of May in 1999, we were at a cottage with some of Vaughan's friends. Vaughan had prepared everything ahead of time for a romantic picnic lunch out on the lake. We enjoyed a nice canoe ride and set up our picnic lunch on a small private island. After we finished eating, he knelt on one knee and asked me to marry him. In my excitement I leaped into his arms! Vaughan replied, "I guess that means yes?" I honestly felt like Vaughan had ridden in on his white horse to save me. I was beginning to live out my happy ending. I looked forward to marrying my knight in shining armour.

♡Chapter 6

An Unexpected Turn!

Vaughan and I were now engaged and I could finally say he was my fiancé. I loved the sound of that. I was so excited to show off my engagement ring and tell people I was getting married.

One week to the day after Vaughan proposed I was getting ready for church. I couldn't wait to get there to tell my friends about our engagement. I remember as I was getting out of the shower that I suddenly began experiencing excruciating pain through my upper back, chest, and arms. It was like nothing I had ever experienced before. I kept trying to shake it off. I kept thinking, "This is a special day and I'm not going to miss it." However, I was unable to get past the pain. Feeling terrified, I struggled to the phone and dialed my parents' number. I tried to calm myself down and explain to them what was happening. I was in such agonizing pain that it was hard for me to even complete a sentence. My parents told me to call 911 and wait for help to arrive. Once the ambulance was on its way, I called Vaughan.

When Vaughan arrived, the paramedics were already carrying me out of my apartment on a stretcher. No one knew what the problem was and they didn't want to take any chances. I kept crying out in pain. Vaughan and I were both really scared. I was rushed to the Peterborough Civic Hospital and given morphine to numb the pain. The drugs helped a little as I lay on a hospital stretcher waiting to see the doctor.

A couple hours had passed when I attempted to roll over and move my leg. I discovered it wasn't working correctly. I had to use my hand to pull it over. When I realized what I was doing, I started to really panic. I shouted for a nurse that was passing by. I didn't understand what was happening and tried to tell her, "I can't seem to move my legs without using my arms." The nurse ran away down the hall to look for help and shortly there was a swarm of activity around my bed. It felt more like a dream--a nightmare really, but this was no dream. Before the end of the day I had lost all movement in my legs and all feeling from my chest down began to disappear. My normal bodily functions stopped. The doctors were afraid that my lungs would also stop and I could no longer breathe. I was rushed to the ICU (Intensive Care Unit) and put on life support.

My pastor in Peterborough called my parents who were visiting my brother Carl in Nova Scotia with the message: "Mr & Mrs. Ings, it doesn't look good. The doctors want you to be prepared because your daughter might not live through the night." My mom and dad immediately drove from Nova Scotia non-stop to Ontario. I cannot imagine how they must have felt as they drove eighteen hours straight with those words replaying in their minds. All the while they were hoping that their daughter would still be alive. They arrived at the hospital totally exhausted and nearly overcome with fear. They were directed to the ICU where they found me hooked up to several machines and a feeding tube. Still alive and in stable condition, I greeted them with tears and a smile, and said, "What took you so long?"

From the very beginning, we had more questions than answers. It was overwhelming for all of us. The paralysis had stopped just below the chest. Then, when the doctors felt it was safe, they allowed me to have visitors. I could only have one at a time as it was too much for me to handle. Specialists were called in and I was placed under constant observation and subjected to numerous tests. However, still no one knew what was happening. On one occasion, while inside this huge MRI scanner, I had an overwhelming sense of fear. I cried out, "God, what do I do? I'm so scared!" I have never heard God's audible voice, but in that moment I felt in my heart I could clearly hear Him say, "I am with you always." God gave me a peace that day that I cannot describe or explain. Knowing God was with me and having the prayers and support of not only my family and friends but even from people I didn't know, I was being supernaturally sustained. I was deeply assured that God was giving me comfort and the support I needed.

I was eventually diagnosed with Transverse Myelitis. The burning question for all of us was, "How did this happen?" We would later understand that this condition is believed to be the result of a viral infection or abnormal immune reaction. You can understand our surprise to discover just how rare it is. The statistic they told us was that only 1 person in every 20 million has this condition. That's probably why no one had any idea of what was happening to me. The doctors were not optimistic about my recovery. After further testing, they felt that even if I were to regain any mobility, I would always require full-time care.

I was totally dependent on the nurses for my daily routine and care. Having to rely on someone else for help was one thing, but needing someone to insert a catheter and assist with your bowel routine on a daily basis was just the most humiliating thing I had ever experienced in my life. Every few hours I would also need two nurses to turn me over to avoid pressure sores. I was totally at the mercy of those entrusted with my care. I couldn't do anything for myself. Even with help, showering was a challenge because I couldn't sit up without support. The nurse would have to fasten me to a special chair and wheel me into the shower.

One particular day after only a few minutes into my shower routine, the nurse assisting me turned away to reach for the shampoo. In that split second I slipped and fell head first toward the shower floor! As I was falling all I could think was, "I'm going to break my neck!" I slapped the wall with my good arm to deflect my head from direct impact and managed to narrowly miss hitting my head. Everything happened so fast! Just as quickly the nurse had me up and secured. She was shaken up as badly as I was and kept apologizing profusely.

For the next few days my hospital roommate said I kept crying out in my sleep, "No! No!" My feeling of utter helplessness was bad enough, but not feeling safe with those entrusted with my care was an overwhelming shock to my emotional stability. I continued to receive heartfelt apologies from that nurse several times a day and anything I needed was brought to me immediately!

The specialist who was assigned to me would come in every day to check on my charts and monitor my progress. He was a great doctor and apparently one of the best in his field. He would come into my room each day, ask me a couple of questions, make some notes, and then leave. I would always greet him with a cheery, "Good morning, Doctor!" and say his name. He was a very serious man and would never laugh at my jokes or acknowledge my cheerfulness, but I never let it affect me. Every day I would try something new to engage him in a friendly conversation or joke. After a while I took this on as a personal challenge to try to get him to smile.

This was no resort or vacation spot but, with flowers all

around me, my room always looked like a flower garden. I looked forward to Vaughan's arrival every evening to wash my face and tuck me in. Each day my mother would braid my hair and complete my look with a flower of choice. One morning when my specialist was making his rounds and documenting my progress I said to him, "So, Doc, would you like a flower for your hair, too?" Much to everyone's amazement, the corner of his lip lifted, as if to crack a smile. The nurse in the room nearly fell over. This was the closest thing to a smile they had seen. Word spread quickly throughout the unit, and I had all these nurses come to me and say, "Wow, you got him to smile?" I can't say that he changed and gave me many more smiles, but that was definitely *one* of my prouder achievements during my hospital stay. (I won't even get into how I managed to have them change all the curtains that surrounded each hospital bed to improve on personal privacy!)

I would often ask my specialist about my condition. I wanted to know what my future was going to look like. He would always be cautious about giving me any type of positive response. I guess he didn't want to be responsible for giving me false hope. Eventually I just stopped asking questions and kept my hope in God. I knew that He was with me and that I was going to be okay.

As I began the long road to recovery and rehabilitation, my daily prayer was that God would give me strength—not only for that day, but often for each hour. As great as it was to have all my family at my side, I knew my father had to return home soon to his church and ministry. On Father's Day, the last weekend before he was to leave, he came to visit me as he always did. As soon as he came into my hospital room, I said, "Dad, Look! Look! I can move my finger!" He began to cry as he told me about a prayer he had just prayed. He said,

"Vahen, today I prayed and asked God to give me a sign that you were going to be okay. I said if I could just see the tip of your finger move, I would be able to leave knowing you would be okay. Coming in today and seeing your finger move was the best Father's Day present a dad could ever have asked for. I can go home now with a greater peace."

We shared a very emotional embrace and thanked God for small blessings. As we sat in the room and talked about that beautiful moment, I couldn't help but say, "You should have asked for the legs too, Dad!" The tears turned into laughter as we continued to thank God. I had many special moments like this with family and friends, and in the midst of all the chaos, I felt so blessed.

Not long after that, I relearned how to apply my own make up. It was so exciting to finally be able to do "something" without help. I was having visitors every day and, if you knew me even a little, you would know that my appearance was important to me. Knowing that, you'll appreciate the humor of picturing me with braids and flowers in my hair with tubes up my nose as my accessories.

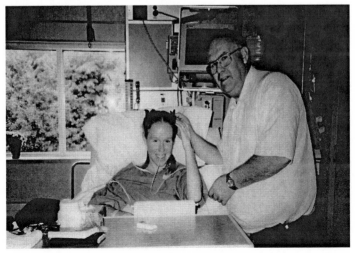

Looking back, I don't think I would have lasted long in the hospital without a sense of humor sandwiched between prayer and support. There was so much for me to consider and, with nothing but time on my hands, I did a lot of thinking as I lay in my hospital bed. It was one of the most physically and emotionally draining experiences I have ever had. My new situation left me unsure about my future. I could remember so well that Sunday morning which now seemed so long ago. I had been filled with such excitement to show everyone my engagement ring. Now I was left wondering: "Would there even be a wedding day?"

♥Chapter 7

An Uncertain Future

In the midst of all the questions and uncertainty, Vaughan had remained faithful and true. He had been visiting me every day without fail, but I still couldn't avoid thinking how everything had now changed since our very recent engagement. Everything about the future felt so uncertain. Up to this point I hadn't even met my future mother and father-in-law. They were missionaries currently serving overseas and wouldn't be returning to Canada for a few more months. Vaughan and I had briefly discussed wedding dates. He had wanted to get married that fall after his parents were back. We had talked to them on the phone several times before and I felt I had bonded well with my soon-to-be in-laws. However, now with this new situation, I wondered if maybe Vaughan or his family may be having second thoughts. For Vaughan to even consider having a wife that may never walk again might be a game changer. How would his parents feel about having a daughter-in-law who had such an extreme disability? To be honest, I didn't feel like wife material. I couldn't even go to the bathroom or shower on my own. How could I expect Vaughan to accept me now?

I just had to talk to Vaughan; he didn't sign up for this. Well, I guess I didn't either, but at least he still had a choice! So when we had some time alone I decided to ask him. "It's been just a short time since we were engaged and we really haven't told many people yet," I said, "so I'd completely understand if you'd like to take this ring back and choose not to marry me." Instead he held my hand and said, "No, Vahen, I love you. God gave you to me. I'm not going to give you back and say you're not good enough!" WOW! I was so amazed. I wasn't sure what to expect, but that was so much better than I could ever have hoped to hear!

Vaughan then shared with me that he had already spoken with his family. They were in full agreement with his decision to continue with our plans to marry and share our future together. I felt true joy and unconditional love. I promised him that I would walk down the aisle on our wedding day. We also knew that my current condition could be a real challenge. Since everything was so uncertain, we decided to postpone our wedding plans for the fall until I was able to be more independent.

Even though I tried very hard, I couldn't get the doctor's assurance that I would ever walk again. I decided to stop asking questions and start focusing on the blessings God was already working in my life. I could not have had better family support. I not only had an amazing man who still wanted me, but his family accepted me unconditionally. When the head nurse heard me repeat my promise made to Vaughan that I would walk down the aisle on our wedding day, she tried to convince my family that I needed to see a doctor--one to assess my mental health. Apparently she thought that I was not thinking clearly or being rational and that I was living in denial.

I clearly remember the day that my specialist came into the room and gave me my diagnosis. His words sounded more like a jury's verdict and a prison sentence. He said, "Vahen, we have determined you have Transverse Myelitis. Since you are still using a feeding tube and unable to sit up on your own, you are not eligible for rehabilitation. We will be keeping you here in the hospital for another two months. After that point you will be transferred to another hospital for full time care and assistance."

I was stunned. I said, "Doctor, I will not be here for two months, and I won't be going into a long-term care facility!" He looked at me and said in his stern voice, "Well, Vahen, these are the facts. Prove them wrong if you can!"

After much questioning and uncertainty, there was a meeting with all the specialists and doctors to determine what my options would be moving forward. Should they send me to a rehabilitation center or into a long-term care facility? In the process of finalizing details about what would happen next, my family doctor at the time spoke up and said, "This girl is only twenty-four years old. What would you do if she were your daughter?" Shortly after that meeting I was told there was an opening for me to go to the rehabilitation hospital in Toronto at the end of the month. However, I needed to be off the feeding tube and sitting up on my own without complications before I could go. In one week, the feeding tube was gone and I was sitting up without getting dizzy. What an exciting moment as I realized I was able to accomplish this goal!

The same nurse who told me I was not thinking clearly would later tell me that I was not strong enough to get out on a day pass to go shopping. She obviously was not privy to my stubborn streak or my love for shopping. One weekend I was determined to get out and buy Vaughan's wedding band. This was something I wanted to do before I left for the rehab centre in Toronto. Before the nurse ended her shift that final Friday before my transfer, she said, "You'll have to wait a little longer, Vahen. I just don't think you're strong enough yet." However, with the help of my mother, we got a cab to the mall where I found the perfect ring for my fiancé.

Monday morning came and I was showing off the ring I had bought. The nurse who was adamant about me not going out that weekend was trying to be happy that I bought the ring, but she just couldn't get past the fact that I "disobeyed" her. (I think that sometimes a little irrational behavior is just what the doctor ordered!)

I'm not sure if I was pushing too hard (or maybe it was that trip to the mall), but a few days later I kept passing out when I tried to sit up. We were worried that they wouldn't send me to rehab if my medical condition was not stable. My mother asked the specialist what was going on. His response was, "Mrs. Ings, I am sorry. I don't know. And not having the answer is sometimes the hardest part of my job."

When you have people supporting you who believe in prayer, losing the chance of rehabilitation was not an option. Five weeks from the time I heard I would be needing full-time care, I was declared stable and ready for discharge! As I was being wheeled out of the hospital to be transferred to Lyndhurst Rehabilitation Centre in Toronto, I spotted my specialist. I couldn't wait to gloat. "Look! I told you I would not be here for two months, and that I was not going into long-term care!" That was another defining moment for me. I stopped listening to what the doctors were saying and trusted in what God was doing. However, for the seven months of intense rehab that followed, I still battled with the thoughts of what my future would look like.

My sister Erica moved to Peterborough from St. John's, Newfoundland, to support me. I was so happy to have her close. I loved my baby sister and wanted to share everything with her. However, when it came time for my physio, I would wonder why there was always somewhere else she had to be. I worked hard and would get so excited about each accomplishment

I was able to achieve such as sitting up and reaching for a cup on the table without falling over. There were many little accomplishments that I wanted to share with her. I remembered that we always enjoyed being together and it made me sad that she wasn't around to celebrate with me. I couldn't understand. It wasn't until I was in Toronto at the rehabilitation centre that I realized the reason for her seeming withdrawal from me. I came to understand that it wasn't that my sister did not want to share in my accomplishments or that she didn't care. Rather, she was struggling with the reality that I was not the vibrant sister she had climbed trees with as a child or had played sports with in high school. In her thinking this just wasn't right. I began to truly understand why my sister felt she couldn't stay at my side. It was just too painful for her to watch me struggle doing the simplest task. She wanted her sister back and she needed time to adjust to this new reality.

I began to see that my road to recovery was going to be much harder than I had originally thought. Reaching for a cup was the least of my worries. I was now struggling to even dress myself without help. The long, slow, and painful process of my daily existence was not easy. Before I could really begin to celebrate one victory, I would be faced with a new challenge. Just a month earlier I couldn't do anything. Then I was eating on my own. Even though I was struggling, I was able to dress myself. I should be excited, right? Yet, every day as I faced the reality of my limitations with even bigger obstacles to overcome, the excitement of my most recent achievements would disappear. My daily personal care and therapy sessions required such intense concentration that I didn't know how I would get through each hour.

I had to remember that I had started out with total paralysis from the chest down and no use of my right arm. Over the weeks we had been seeing constant improvements in my health. I had to try and focus on how far I have come and not on how far I had to go. I had to acknowledge that I was gaining more independence all the time. I could now shower, use the bathroom, and dress myself. I had even taken a few trips out to the mall in my power chair. Daily workouts pushed my limits farther every day. Yes it was slow, but I was encouraged by the new progress.

The rehabilitation centre was in Toronto, about an hour and a half drive from Peterborough. It was on a large secluded property with cultivated grounds in the middle of a busy city. There were dorm wings that felt like a hospital with 3 or 4 beds in a room and curtains in between each. The beds were hospital beds and the nurses would be in and out of your room all hours of the day or night to help with any physical needs. There was a cafeteria, a large gym, a physio pool and workout facility, as well as a library with computer access for emails or internet use.

There were over 100 patients when I was there, all with different issues and stages of rehabilitation. I remember one gentleman in a power chair who was fearless. He only knew 2 speeds in his chair: top speed with the front wheels off the ground or stop. The nurses finally had to put a speed governor on his chair to slow him down so he wouldn't cause an accident with the other patients or visitors!

It was pretty busy during the week with working out and taking care of the daily routines. Visitors would sometimes come by in the evenings or on weekends. Vaughan would drive down every weekend to spend time with me. We would go out and enjoy the scenic park-like grounds, play some board games in the recreation room, cuddle on the bed watching my little 6" TV, or even take small side trips into the city just to feel normal and get away from the hospital atmosphere of the centre.

After 4 or 5 months, I hit a plateau with my rehabilitation. There wasn't enough new progress each week for them to justify their time and effort. It was suggested by my therapist that I probably wouldn't see much more improvement. Of course this was a major disappointment. I was trying my best, but that wasn't enough to stay on. I didn't even try to fight it. I had reached a point where I was sick of living in a hospital environment and I wanted to get on with my life. I decided to focus on the things I could do and not waste time on what I couldn't. I felt I had achieved enough independence to live on my own. I began to focus on my wedding day and walking down that aisle. Looking forward to my future with Vaughan, I started to plan our wedding day.

♡ *Chapter 8*

My First Big Steps

It was finally here. The day I had dreamed and fantasized about since I was a young girl. My wedding day. My mother told me that I was always a dreamer and desired the best. She said, "Vahen, that is a great quality, because God desires to give us His best." Anytime I would talk about my wedding I would always say I wanted a fairy-tale wedding. However, the way the events had unfolded in my life, I felt that dream would never happen. But today my dream was now my reality. God gave me this amazing man and now he was about to become my husband.

However, in all my fantasies about my wedding day, being in a wheelchair had definitely not been a part of my plans. Originally I had told Vaughan that I wasn't going to get married until I was out of this wheelchair. We had, however, made the decision to set the date for early May, the year 2000, but I didn't know how I would make this happen. My mind was just stuck on what a "normal" wedding looked like. I wondered if that dream would ever happen. But my mother quickly reminded me that this was *my* day, and I could plan it any way I wanted. Just hearing that and knowing that I had the freedom to do whatever I wanted alleviated a lot of my stress.

The majority of our friends and family who were part of

our wedding party had arrived in Newfoundland a few days before the big day. Vaughan and I had gone a week before the wedding to get settled and finalize last minute details. My parents met us at the airport. And, finally my parents were able to meet Vaughan's family for the first time. Following the wedding rehearsal, I was able to have a heart-to-heart conversation with my mother. She shared some of her thoughts and concerns with me.

She said, "Vahen, at the rehearsal Vaughan's parents just did everything so naturally and fit in so well with everyone. Their only concern was your happiness and comfort. They obviously have totally accepted you and your disability. I could definitely tell it wasn't an act."

She continued, "It was a very emotional time for us as your father and I contemplated walking you down the aisle. We had doubts about handing you over to Vaughan. Could he love you as much as we did? Could he provide your needs now that you were in a wheelchair? Could his family accept you as we did-- unconditionally? But, as I looked at the bridal party, at Vaughan's family, and at his friends who had come to celebrate with us, my doubts vanished. I knew this was real. It was then that I realized how much this family showed real love to you and our family. I have no doubts, Vahen, but that you have found a love that would last."

I also had the best bridal party anyone could ask for. My attendants were my sister, Vaughan's sister and two of my good friends. The groomsmen were Vaughan's dad, his brother, cousin, and a good friend. They went all out with decorating the reception hall the night before. They even insisted that I go home to rest while they stayed on to make sure everything was completed. That really helped with handling the stress of the big day!

As I awoke to my wedding day I was really trying not to focus on all the things that could go wrong. However, one thing that still concerned me was the fact that I was going to be walking down the aisle in a big puffy wedding dress. I hadn't been able to rehearse for that, so my nerves were running high. Still concerned, but trying to not focus on the "what if's," I headed off to the salon with the other girls in my bridal party for our beauty rituals.

As I was sitting in the salon chair, it was really sinking in: it's here—my wedding day! A day I thought that would never happen was now my reality. God gave me this amazing man and now he was about to become my husband. I pictured the moment when Vaughan would first see me. I really wanted to wow and surprise him as I walked down the aisle. I wanted to be the beautiful bride that he would be proud of. Right then, the salon door opened and a delivery man walked in holding a beautiful bouquet of roses. They were from my amazing husband-to-be. What a tender and timely expression of his love and commitment to me. Up until that time I had been too focused to cry. But, when I saw those flowers and realized his thoughts and his heart were with me, I started to feel the tears coming. I had to quickly compose myself as the girls reminded me not to ruin my make-up! After a few hours, we left the salon looking beautiful and ready to finish the final touches before heading to the church.

It wasn't until I was in my dress and ready to head to church that I fully realized how impossible it would have been to wheel around in my wheelchair with this big dress on. I was so glad that I planned not to use the wheelchair during the ceremony. Just getting out of the building to the car was a chore in itself. I needed two of my bridesmaids to hold my dress as I was wheeled out through the door.

We arrived at the church and were ready to start the service right on time when I heard my mom say, "Vahen. Where is your bouquet?" We all looked at each other and realized we had forgotten my beautiful flowers! My mom quickly insisted that my brother drive back to the hotel and get my wedding bouquet.

Half an hour later everything was in place. The wedding party all took their positions. With my bouquet finally in hand, we were ready to begin. I heard the music intro start and my heart began to race. As I watched my bridesmaids walk down the aisle one at a time, I prayed, "Dear God, please don't let me fall!" It seemed like only seconds later and it was my turn. The wedding song started to play and I was sitting in my chair right at the entrance to the auditorium with the doors closed. I gave the okay signal and the doors were opened for me. With my dad holding one arm and my mom holding the other, I stood to my feet and made my way down the aisle. I don't remember anything about that walk other than the fact that my only focus was making it down the aisle and keeping my eyes on Vaughan to see his reaction. It was not my most graceful walk as I even stumbled a little, but it was all just fine because I was *doing it*. (In fact, it was a miracle!) I looked up at Vaughan and as I saw the emotion on his face, I knew that he was wowed and so impressed to see me walk down that aisle. I felt beautiful and truly loved.

We reached the end of the aisle and my dad attempted to pick me up and place me in this beautifully decorated chair at the front of the church facing Vaughan. As he did so, the train of my gown pushed against the chair and tipped it over. I remember feeling so embarrassed as my dad was holding me and trying to pick up the chair at the same time. But, as soon as I got settled and looked at Vaughan, I quickly forgot anything I may have felt was going wrong. I was about to sing a solo to my soul mate. As the music began, I focused only on Vaughan as I sang "From This Moment," by Shania Twain[4].

---

4 "From This Moment On" by Canadian recording artist Shania Twain, "Come On Over" (1997).

Vaughan couldn't stop smiling and sniffling as he tried to hold back the tears. I could see the pride and love in his eyes. In that moment it seemed that we were the only ones in that room. Later, my mother-in-law said to me, "Vahen, you sang so beautifully and didn't even falter. I don't think there was a dry eye in the auditorium. I was sobbing so loudly I thought they could hear me in the next building!"

When the song was over, my dad lifted me out of the chair and brought me to where Vaughan was standing. The pastor who was doing the first part of the ceremony began, "Who gives this woman to be married to this man?" My dad replied, "I do," and then literally lifted me up and put me into Vaughan's arms. Vaughan then placed me onto another beautifully decorated chair beside him. We held hands in front of our friends and family and began to exchange our wedding vows.

For this part of the service my dad, being a pastor, was the officiating minister and continued the marriage ceremony. I was feeling so much love for Vaughan as we declared our commitment to each other and exchanged our vows. My dad read the vows and we repeated after him. Right at the end of the vows as Vaughan was repeating the final phrase after my father, he paused and asked, "What? Can you repeat that please?" So again my dad said, "And thereto I plight thee my troth." Vaughan didn't understand the word 'troth' and thought maybe he hadn't understood my father's "newfie" accent. So with that he stepped up to my dad, took the book from his hand, and looked at what he was supposed to say. Apparently "troth" was actually the real word. So, Vaughan handed the book back to my dad and repeated the final vow to the congregation. It was so embarrassing yet one of the funniest moments I had ever experienced. Later at the reception when he was giving his speech, Vaughan explained to everyone that he thought he misunderstood the "newfie" accent and he wanted to know what he was giving up. To this day that still gets us laughing.

After we finished exchanging our vows, we moved on to lighting the unity candle and to the signing of the registry. Vaughan's cousin Jason (the best man) and my sister Erica (my maid of honor) moved these items to where we were seated. Then, as Vaughan and I said our final "I do's," Vaughan picked me up in his arms and we walked out of the church with everyone cheering and applauding. Vaughan really was my knight in shining armour who had literally swept me off my feet. To this day when people ask me "What happened to you? Why are you in a wheelchair?" My response is, "My husband asked me to marry him and he literally swept me off my feet." I thought it was a fun way to answer."

When Vaughan and I were in the back of the car on our way to have our pictures taken, I looked down and was shocked to see white socks peeking out from under his black pants. In a loud, scolding tone, I said, "Vaughan! Why are you wearing white socks?" He paused and pretended for a moment that he didn't know any better. I was appalled and said, "Please tell me you knew you are supposed to wear black socks with that tuxedo?" He started to laugh as he explained to me that one of his groomsmen suggested they play a prank on me and thought it would be cool for all of the groomsmen to have a group picture showing off their white socks. I was relieved to know that my husband was not totally clueless when it came to fashion!

As everyone knows, the maid of honor gets the major task of assisting the bride with whatever she needs for that day. One of the most daunting tasks that I requested of my maid of honor and one of the biggest blessings for me came at the reception when it was time for me to go to the ladies' room. You can only imagine how difficult it was with that big wedding dress! Just like the trooper she was, my sister held up my dress as I took care of business. That's true love and dedication right there!

As delightful as the whole day was, I was getting more and more exhausted as the evening went on. In the middle of the speeches and toasts, my brother Carl, who was master of ceremonies, turned to me and asked, "How much longer do you want to keep the speeches going, Sis?" He had been doing a tremendous job of keeping the guests happy and entertained, but I was feeling so tired. I think I had reached the point where I couldn't get out of there fast enough. I assured him that I was quite content and it was definitely okay to wrap up the program. I knew if I didn't get out of there soon I would have nothing left for the wedding night, and that wasn't acceptable.

For our honeymoon, Vaughan and I toured around the parts of Newfoundland where I grew up. He hadn't seen much of the island, so I was happy to spend the next week showing him where I came from and enjoying a road trip together.

There were many times along the way when Vaughan would just pull over to the side of the road and climb a rock and take a picture of the scenery. However, one time when he was out on this beaten down old wharf (that's the "newfie" term for a dock), there were broken planks and holes on it in places. It looked a little unstable when Vaughan was walking out on it. He was halfway out when I started screaming, "Vaughan! Vaughan! Come back!" As he attempted to tell me he was okay, I keep screaming, "No! Come quickly! There is a bee in the car!" He ran back to assist me, but he teased me saying, "I thought my wife was so concerned for my safety that she was frantically calling me back, but it turns out she's just scared of a bee!"

Vaughan and I were beginning our life together a little differently than most young married couples. Now that we were married and finally together, we assumed that most of our problems would be behind us. We were young, in love, and ready to take on the world together.

♡ **Chapter 9**

The Challenges

Vaughan and I were one of those couples that everyone looked at and said, "Now there's the picture of a happy couple." I really objected to people saying, "Just wait until you get out of your three-year honeymoon phase!" I wanted to say, "That's not us; we are going to be happy forever!" I don't think anyone wants to hear that you only have unhappiness to look forward to. Vaughan and I realized it wasn't always going to be all rosy and wonderful. We knew we would have to adjust to many new situations just like any other newlywed couple.

We both soon discovered that we weren't only dealing with the challenges of being newlyweds; we were also adapting to how my disability fit into our marriage. I remember on many occasions I would struggle with trying to find the balance between being independent and allowing my husband to treat me like a lady. Do I let him do everyday things for me like getting the doors, etc? Or do I show him how independent I am by attempting all these things on my own to prove I can? I really thought it was better for both of us if I showed him how independent I could be.

For the next three years Vaughan worked and supported us while I continued to strengthen my body with weekly physio sessions. This was one area that I had no control over and I had to rely on Vaughan. I wasn't able to work just yet and didn't know how that would affect us, but at the time we just kept doing what we could. Unfortunately, one month before I was hospitalized, I had purchased a small car to travel between my two part-time jobs. Now I couldn't drive and we had no need for a second vehicle. We took it back to the dealership to sell for us. This was before Kijiji and online classifieds became the norm, so I was stuck with making car payments until it finally sold a year later.

I also remember that from the very first weeks in the hospital, I was receiving calls from the bank about my student loan payments. In the best of times these calls are taxing, but in the middle of intense rehabilitation, it was just too much to handle. I signed permission for my mother to deal with the banks on my behalf. That didn't seem to work because I continued to get call after call about my repayments. They were not adhering to my request to speak to my mother. Not only were they still calling me, but they were also accusing me of faking my story to avoid payments. I would literally be in tears before they would let me get off the phone.

My mother gathered all the documents of my condition and kept submitting them to the bank where my loans were held. We requested that they put these loans on hold until I was able to work again. It was a long and drawn out process, but finally, after two years of fighting, my student loan that was worth almost $30,000 was forgiven. This was an amazing blessing. It took a huge financial weight off our shoulders, but it seemed we were still living from paycheck to paycheck.

As Vaughan and I struggled to overcome these new challenges and transitions, I don't think either of us really grasped the full reality of the situation and how it slowly started to erode our relationship. Facing daily physical and emotional barriers became my new reality and now there was the constant struggle with feeling less than beautiful sitting in a wheelchair. However, never once did I think that my spiritual foundation would be shaken so much.

We attended several healing services, believing that God would finish the healing I felt had started in my body. Repeatedly we would leave feeling disappointed and discouraged. One evangelist actually told me that God wanted to heal me, but that I should come back on Wednesday night. As crazy as that sounds now, I did feel anticipation the rest of the week as I waited for Wednesday to come. As the Wednesday night service was coming to a close, the evangelist approached me and said that tonight was not my night, but he had a scripture for me: Matthew 6:33. "But seek first the kingdom of God and His righteousness, and all these things shall be added to you." I left that night speechless and confused, but in my heart I was asking the question, "What did he mean?" The last time God gave me that scripture I was five years old and He showed me that I could have both. Did it mean something different now? I questioned God and said "God, I have committed my whole life to you and have always loved you. Am I not good enough?" I was left feeling hurt and more confused than ever. Didn't God want to heal me?

It seemed there were many people who felt they knew what God was trying to tell me. On one occasion I was invited to attend a home meeting with a group of people who wanted to believe for my healing. Their motto was: "If you have enough faith, God will heal you." I was told I needed to get serious with God and crawl on the floor and refuse to use my chair. It would get God's attention and show Him my faith and He would heal me. I remember crawling on my hands and knees and crying while people were holding me and pushing me along, but I didn't receive any healing.

Other people started to question me: "Perhaps there is unconfessed sin in your life that is holding you back from God." I started thinking that maybe they were right. Maybe I did have sin in my life that was standing between me and God. What could I do to change this? I didn't know how to confess any differently. I begged God to show me what I needed to do.

When I didn't receive any answers, I began to think, "I know I'm not perfect, but would God really punish me like this?" What about the relationship I had with God when I was five, when I knew Him to be a forgiving God who loves me unconditionally? How could I have forgotten that? Instead of going to God as I had always done, I began to allow the viewpoint of others to override my relationship with Him. I started to become angry at God and all things that were said and done in His name.

Sometimes I would be talking with Vaughan and crying because it all seemed so impossible. As much as I knew he was trying to understand, he just couldn't. He wanted me to be strong and not cry about it. He tried to be encouraging, but I realize now that he couldn't handle all these emotions. It was overwhelming to him (and me). At that point I started to move on and repress the hurts I was feeling. I needed to find my strength and independence, but I was confused about what that meant now. I started believing that to cry was to be weak and independence meant that I couldn't turn to my husband in time of need.

My heart was becoming tainted with bitterness and resentment, partly because I was in a wheelchair, but also because I couldn't seem to communicate with my husband. I started to believe that my God was not a loving God. If I heard one more person say, that "All things work together for good to them that love God", I swear I was going to punch them in the face. I had thought that living life as a person with a disability was going to be my toughest challenge, but nothing was farther from the truth.

Every Sunday at church it seemed I heard; "Well, there's the happy couple!" "Why aren't you walking yet?" "Have more faith." But my very favorite was, "Don't worry, all things work together for good to them that love God." I wanted to scream. Not walking was the least of my worries. All I wanted was comfort for what I was feeling inside, but people were more concerned with my outside. I retreated farther into my pain by blocking my feelings. All the while I was trying to appear "normal."

I was still going to church with Vaughan, but I felt people saw me as a project they had to fix. I was hurting on the inside and needed prayer to help with all the emotions I was dealing with. Yet, when I would go up to the front of the church to open my heart to God, people would just start praying for my physical healing. They assumed that's what I was there for. I know they wanted to help, but they couldn't see beyond my physical disability.

The church we were involved in was going through some divisive changes. Vaughan and I were asked to help out by taking on more responsibilities. We thought it was the "right thing to do." We made the mistake of thinking that more involvement equaled more fulfillment. We were serving because we were asked and needed, rather than from an inner passion of love from God's Spirit. We were serving every Sunday at church but our spirits weren't being refilled. Instead of keeping a balance between our personal and spiritual lives, we ended up feeling overextended in our church ministry and we just burned out. We didn't want to complain or tell anyone what we were feeling, so we eventually stopped going. We now found ourselves living in a frustrating combination of multiplied challenges which were eroding our peace with God and each other.

♡Chapter 10

Hitting Rock Bottom

The disappointing events that now had become part of our lives left scars on my heart. I became really good at masking my hurts. I also had fears about intimacy with Vaughan. I struggled with the physical limitations in my body; my lack of feeling physical touch and sensation was definitely a big one. I wondered just how much longer it would be before I could feel anything except mild sensations. In some areas, it was like touching your arm through your jacket, as opposed to touching your bare arm. The feeling was dulled. Then there were areas that I couldn't feel touch at all. I couldn't tell if something was hot, cold, or sharp. I couldn't trust my capacity to feel pain. I would always be afraid of placing a knife or even an unplugged iron in my lap as I moved around the house.

I was devastated that Vaughan and I couldn't have that strong physical connection that we should have been able to have. Even on our wedding night, I prayed that God would let me feel my husband's touch. Vaughan was a caring husband and tried so hard to meet my physical needs. He knew there was some loss and limitation of feeling. But, I didn't want him to feel bad about something he couldn't do anything about. I made the choice to hide how much sensation I truly had and just pretended to be normal. I suppressed this to hide how I truly felt.

Even though I was hurt by frequent comments from people regarding my healing, my greatest turmoil was the whole whirlwind of emotions and feelings I couldn't process or understand. I devoted almost all of my time in those first few years focusing on rehabilitation. After I had stopped seeing any improvements in my body, I stopped going to physiotherapy. Instead of focusing on what I couldn't do, I decided to focus on what I could do and simply make the best of it.

One of the first things I wanted to do was start driving again. I saw many people with far less mobility than I had, successfully driving and living life. So, after much looking around, I found a used car in Toronto that already had hand controls installed. The gentleman who sold it to me was also in a wheelchair and was upgrading to a newer vehicle. My new car cost me $500 and was a big 8-cylinder Oldsmobile with a long bench seat in the front. I would transfer myself into the passenger side of the car and pull the chair in behind me. Before I scooted over behind the steering wheel, I would pull this long strap that was tied to the door handle to close it. The car was horrible on gas, but it was my first big step toward regaining my independence.

Our next challenge was finding an accessible apartment building with underground parking. Above-ground parking wasn't really an option because I couldn't wheel my chair through the winter snow without help. Every building that had underground parking seemed to have some kind of accessibility issue. There would always be a step or other obstacle blocking the route into the building. We finally found the one building in the city that could be considered somewhat accessible, but the whole underground garage floor was on a steep slope. The best parking spot available was about halfway up the indoor hill, but I needed the strength of Hercules to push myself up that incline. Then I had to pry open the fireproof door with one hand while I attempted to wheel myself backwards with my other hand until the door was open wide enough for me to slip inside. (People would often admire the muscles in my arms, but I doubt they understood the workouts I had to do each day just to achieve that!) Once I got to the elevator, I was home free!

The next step towards more independence was going back to work. I found a full time job working in a computer support call centre. I was definitely not the technical type, but they liked my personality and were eager to teach me the rest. After an intense training phase, I now had a job. I held my own with the basic troubleshooting, but my manager was always impressed that I had no problem selling upgrades or handling the irritated customers. I was happy to have a job and my own income. More importantly, I felt I was doing something productive again. At first I was really happy working there, but as time went on I could see the huge turnover rate. It was a high stress environment and people would often leave or just quit. The customers we were assisting would often make or break your day. It was just not the best working environment for me. I started becoming more negative as well and dreading my time at work. My negativity began spilling over into so many areas of my life.

Of course this negative attitude was not helping Vaughan and I with our communication. In fact, our communication was becoming more and more limited. We didn't see what was happening at the time, but our lack of communication and negative attitude were causing us to drift farther apart. Vaughan had gotten involved in an online game. It was one of those games where you played forever and you still would not finish it. Building up his online character was a full time endeavor. He seemed to be always sitting in front of the computer with a headset on talking to his "buddies." We started to immerse ourselves into our own worlds bit by bit. At this point we had left God behind and I was working odd and late shifts at the call centre. We had this seemingly impenetrable wall between us that I did not know how to remove.

Through our crazy mix of emotions (or maybe it was a lack of the right kind of emotions) we thought it was a good idea to try to begin our family. It wasn't long before we found out I was two months pregnant. We were having a baby! This was a new life, a new focus, and a new beginning.

Not long after receiving this amazing news everything changed. It was 10:30 pm and Vaughan was in bed getting some rest. He was flying out to California for a trade show early the next morning with his boss. I was in the bathroom when I started bleeding. I couldn't grasp what was happening. Was I losing our baby? Crying uncontrollably, I called the provincial health services help line, Health Link.

After speaking with Health Link, I was advised to get to a hospital immediately. Vaughan woke up and rushed me to the hospital. After what seemed like an eternity, the doctor confirmed that yes, I was having a miscarriage, and that it appeared as though we might have had twins. I was in shock--not only because of the loss we had just experienced, but also by Vaughan's lack of emotion to what was happening. His way of comforting me was to say "Oh well, it was too early to have developed very far. Don't worry; we can try again later." He seemed more concerned that he would let his boss down or miss his flight than how I was feeling. It was all too much to process. I wanted Vaughan to understand how much I needed him, but I didn't know how to communicate my feelings. I was numb.

We arrived home from the hospital at 3 a.m. and Vaughan was out the door half an hour later to catch his flight for the two-week business trip. I could not grasp the fact that he could leave me home alone in the middle of this time of crisis. What was he thinking? How could he? Was he not sad we lost our baby? Yes, I know I could have said, "Sweetie, I need you. Please stay," but I needed *him* to say he wanted to stay. I actually felt I was an inconvenience to his plans. I never felt more alone than I did in that moment. I felt abandoned by both my husband and God.

My decision to not rely on my husband for emotional support was a decision I never regretted more than I did in that moment. My family was devastated by the news of the miscarriage and equally confused about Vaughan's behavior. That day my sister called and asked if Vaughan was with me. I said, "No. He left for a business trip." I started to cry. Erica dropped everything to be there with me and try to comfort me through this emotional mess. I love my sister and I will be forever thankful for the time she spent with me. Looking back, I really don't think I would have made it through those first couple days without her there.

It was years later that my sister and I discussed that visit. From her point of view, she remembered that I seemed to be minimizing the entire loss. She felt I was discounting it all as "no big thing" and wondered if she should have even come. However, she said she quickly realized that I was so numb to everything that I would really need her help to figure out what to do next. She suggested that I take a little time off work. At first I didn't think that was necessary, but she helped me see that I was choosing to just not deal with my hurt and was keeping everything inside. She printed off forms for me to take to my doctor so that I could be off work for a few months. I would never have made the decision without her. I was thankful that she was there for me at a time when I didn't know what I needed or wanted. I had very little capacity to even discuss the pregnancy. Somehow by keeping quiet I felt I was holding back the flood of sorrow, loss, and pain that seemed to threaten to swallow me up. Our conversations were mostly void of that direct topic. About a year later after the miscarriage when Erica and I were talking, I showed her a few things I bought while I was pregnant. She later reflected on that incident: "Vahen, that was the first time you had ever really talked about the pregnancy. You told me that the doctor said it looked like you may have had twins. It was nice to finally hear you talk about it."

After my sister had left and only days after the miscarriage, I still had follow-up appointments at the hospital. But, hey, I was used to being independent and doing things for myself. So, I didn't even plan to ask for help. However, my mother-in-law called and said, "Your father-in-law and I felt that I should come and take you to your appointments." I felt like I was on autopilot. I know I could not have made it without the support I was given. I don't think she will ever fully understand just how much I appreciated her being there for me.

When the appointments were done and I was left alone to let it all sink in, I found myself at the most vulnerable point of my life and my marriage. I wanted more. I wanted a man who could love me back and communicate with me. I realized later that it was at that point when I emotionally checked out of our marriage. We continued living under the same roof, but there was no communication and, sadly, no love. It felt like we were living as roommates rather than husband and wife. The silence was deafening.

Any woman wants to feel special and be treated like a lady. She feels so secure and special to have her man hold the door or say, "Yes, Honey, let me get that for you." These may all sound like little things, but they were things that I was missing because I was trying to prove my independence. In contrast to my hours at home, once at work I was viewed as a cool gal in a wheelchair. I enjoyed challenging people's perceptions of what a person with a disability "looked like" and it gave me a sense of pride. I started to enjoy my new-found independence and the attention I was getting. I was becoming more self-reliant rather than relying on my husband.

It became easy to open up to my new friends who seemed to have just as many problems as I did. I told them the truth about my marriage and what I was dealing with. I knew this was a bad choice, but I just didn't seem to care anymore. I knew that talking to other people and especially other men outside my marriage for emotional support was leading me into dangerous territory. I was fooling myself into thinking that this was okay. The more I pulled away from Vaughan, the more appealing these relationships became. This led me to make my biggest mistake of all—I allowed myself to fall into an extra-marital affair. How did I get here? I had always cherished my relationship with Vaughan, and yet now I'm rejecting him and everything I ever believed in.

I was feeling trapped in my life and started to push everyone away. I built a whole secret life of sin around me. But, it began to cave in on me. God didn't care about me. Vaughan obviously didn't care; and, to be honest, I really didn't care what happened to my life either. I believed I had ruined any plans that God had for me and that I was no longer worthy of His love. Experiencing God's love and the love of my husband again was a fairy-tale ending not meant for me.

How could I expect God to heal my heart and my marriage now after all the hurt and pain I had caused? And, to make it all worse, I held God responsible for it. I knew Vaughan wanted a God-fearing wife, and I was nothing like the woman he chose to spend his life with. I really believed that I had committed an unforgivable sin, and that I had to let Vaughan go. In my quest to find a way out, I told him I was seeing someone else and that I wanted out of our marriage. I even told him I was looking for another place to live.

Vaughan was shocked! He had no idea I had been living this secret life. It was a very emotional conversation. He had assumed we were just taking a break from church and pulling back from our responsibilities to regain some sense of balance. But in my mind, we were barely hanging on. I had become so good at hiding my feelings and emotions from him. Life had become just one mundane day after another: work all day, come home, eat dinner, have Vaughan return to hanging out with his online friends, and repeat.

With my announcement of the infidelity, everything changed. Vaughan was very upset about my affair and betrayal and needed some space. He packed a small bag and left to go stay with his parents. Before he left he said he needed time apart to think and clear his head and that we could talk in a week. At that point I wasn't sure what I was feeling. I wanted to break free of Vaughan and anyone close to me. I needed to start over. I wanted to get away from this numbness and just feel something other than this deep, deep loneliness. I had hurt Vaughan and pushed him away and now I was feeling very alone. I had no idea what the future was going to hold.

This was not the life I had set out to live! I had been wandering from one bad choice to another. The next few days were even more difficult as I realized that I had hit rock bottom and I didn't know how to get back up. Honestly, I felt like someone had just removed my conscience and crushed my moral compass. Who was this person that I had become? This really scared me, because deep down I knew that Vaughan was the man God gave me. If he walked away, I knew I would never be truly happy again. I had no control over what was to happen next.

After about 3 days Vaughan called me. He wanted to come see me and talk. He picked me up and we drove somewhere quiet where we just sat and talked for hours. He wasn't angry anymore, but he completely opened up and listened to me. Vaughan explained that over the last few days he had struggled deeply with the bitterness of betrayal and the depth of his anger towards me. However, he also came to understand how he had failed me by not recognizing how much I was hurting. Even though he had a choice to leave me and to never talk to me again, he really felt that we were brought together for a reason. He continued to say "When I married you, it was for life. I'm sorry I left you alone when you lost our baby. I will do whatever it takes to fix this. Are you willing to do the same?"

I then had a flashback of Vaughan's words to me when I first got sick: "God gave you to me and I'm not going to give you back now and say you're not good enough." As we sat in that car in that quiet place with the first true communication we had known for a long while, I don't remember what I was feeling or even if I said anything at that point. But, I could clearly feel Vaughan's sincerity when he said, "We will get through this together."

Did I feel love and forgiveness right away? No, I felt nothing but hurt, resentment, unworthiness, and guilt. Trust me when I say it wasn't easy. Vaughan and I obviously had some major trust issues to work through, and although communication was not our strength, I told him I would stay and commit to work on our relationship, our marriage, and our future together.

I knew that without God's help this would be a tough road. Even though I was not serving God, I had lots to say to Him. Many times I pleaded with Him, "God, you have to change my heart or let me go. I do not have peace. I need to know there is more to life than this constant turmoil." I wanted to trust myself and love Vaughan, but I could not let go of the guilt and pain I had held on to for so long. And now, all of this was compounded by the shame I was feeling. Yes, I had made the bold and decisive step of breaking the relationship with the man with whom I had committed adultery. Yet, the internal struggle I experienced daily was just too much. Was it possible for me to let go and be free? If I couldn't forgive myself, how could I believe that God or my husband could ever forgive me?

Vaughan and I went for counseling to talk about the miscarriage. Through counseling, I also came to realize that I had never allowed myself to mourn the loss of my health. I held this all inside. I was in denial about the loss I had experienced, but was unable to communicate what I was feeling. I began to doubt and pull away from God even more. Why would He allow me to hurt this way? I wanted more than anything to be that compassionate woman with a heart for God. Where was she? Would I ever find my way back? What about all the hopes and dreams I had for my future? I was convinced that my "penance" was to stay unhappy and just cope with my life.

In attempts to rebuild our marriage, Vaughan and I started making a few changes. First of all, the environment where I was working was not helping our fragile relationship, especially since the man whom I had the affair with was at my workplace. It made my decision to leave more necessary. If there was going to be a chance for us to repair our relationship, I knew I had to quit. Vaughan gave up his computer habits and started to focus more on our relationship. Finances were tight now with only one income so Vaughan began seriously looking into other job opportunities. We had heard that it was easy to get a decent paying job out west, so he contacted some of his old friends who were living in Alberta. This would give us an opportunity to start over and would restore a sense of hope. After that encouraging contact, it didn't take long for us to make the decision to move. Would it really be possible for us to make a new start in a new place?

♡ *Chapter 11*

God's Intervention

Within weeks of moving to Alberta, Vaughan and I both found excellent jobs. We had a new start with a positive outlook. He was hired on with an electrical company and I started working in a large bank's call centre.

Vaughan and I began to communicate more openly about our feelings. At first it was frightening to be that honest and vulnerable. However, the fact that we were communicating at all was a positive turn in our relationship. We started growing closer and began to see that it was possible to fall in love again. This healing process did not happen overnight. It was a challenge at times to let go of the pain and disappointments, but it was necessary in order to move forward. Our open communication throughout the years that followed brought about much emotional healing.

I remember one day Vaughan and I were relaxing and having a little talk when we got a call from a friend. She told me the tragic news that she had just miscarried and lost their baby. After I relayed this awful news to Vaughan, he said, "Oh that is just terrible! They must be going through so much pain right now; I cannot imagine what they must be feeling."

I quickly remembered what I had gone through almost three years before with the miscarriage. "Vaughan, you know that is exactly what happened to me, right?" I had never seen Vaughan so moved to tears as he was that day. He immediately embraced me and said, "Sweetie, I am so sorry! I am so sorry! Please forgive me. I never would have left you alone had I realized you were in that much pain." Then he asked me to share with him all about the events of that day and what I had gone through. For the next hour I relived every moment of the night I had the miscarriage including when the doctor said, "I think you might have had twins." Vaughan said, "Sweetie, please forgive me for leaving you on your own after we returned from the hospital following the miscarriage. I will never want you to feel that alone and abandoned ever again. And twins? I would have loved to have had twins."

People may commonly say that time heals all wounds. However, before Vaughan and I truly felt whole, it was not merely time alone that brought healing, but time and many tough conversations. Moving on and rebuilding love and trust was a painful process that took a lot of time and effort. I actually told Vaughan that I felt that the sin I carried in my life was like the freckles on my body. It was a part of me.

Over the next few years Vaughan and I did have struggles and it wasn't always easy, but our communication and relationship progressively grew stronger. He was more open to listening to me and discussing feelings and emotions without jumping in and trying to fix things. We found a balance. I realized his emotional tank wasn't as big as mine so I was careful not to overwhelm him with too much all at once. We were growing closer together, developing new friendships, and starting promising careers.

During these first few years in Alberta I still had a large part of my heart blocked from God. I didn't trust myself to open up to Him and I wasn't ready to face church people again. Vaughan, on the other hand, was going to church with one of his buddies that he met at work while I would stay home. He didn't push God or the restoration of my relationship with God and I was thankful for that.

In my heart though, I often reflected on the passion I had for God when I was a teenager. I would often wonder how I got to where I was now. One day as I was looking through Facebook, I saw that one of my good friends I had known since grade one was moving to Alberta. I couldn't believe my eyes. She had always known me as a kind, compassionate person who loved the Lord. Now look at me! Struck with fear, I thought, "Oh dear, she's going to see the terrible person I have become." Then I wondered if maybe God was sending her into my postal code to help me somehow. My mind was racing. I was so afraid to hope, but I couldn't help but be drawn to her. Very soon after that I made contact, and we did reconnect.

On February 5, 2011, Vaughan and I went to visit my friend and her husband. She spoke about the amazing things God was doing in her life. In contrast, I couldn't help but express how angry I was at Him. I couldn't understand why God would allow me to become so cold and empty. I thought God had given up on me. Before we left their home that night, my friend prayed for God to heal my heart and my body. I thought, "Whatever! God doesn't care about me anymore." My insensitive remark was, "Yeah, good luck with that. And oh, if God does heal me, He'd better let me walk in heels."

Later that night, I had a dream that changed my life. I dreamt that I was able to walk, but I was very bitter and angry at God. I was telling my dad how upset I was at God. I thought that He had turned His back on me, and I was so scared. Inside, I was yelling but I could not speak His name out loud. I woke up sobbing as I remembered all the hurts of my not-so-distant past. Abruptly, though, I stopped crying because I thought,

"What's the point of my tears? They have gotten me nowhere." Fear gripped me. I truly wanted God to change my heart, but I was so afraid to trust Him. I thought I had lost all hope. In that moment, the Lord began reminding me of the many blessings in my life. These were blessings I could not deny. He reminded me of my husband's perseverance and commitment to keep our marriage through its darkest hour. He also reminded me how He was always there for me and wanted to be there for me now. He reminded me of my calling in life to impact the world for Him.

With tears trickling down my face I prayed, "Okay God, I want this cycle to stop. I want to trust you. I need to be free from the sin and guilt that has gripped my heart and my marriage." Could I really be a faithful wife and love Vaughan the way I knew he should be loved? Could I really let go of this hidden, sinful lifestyle? I was afraid to hope. I did not want to be let down by hoping for things from God that would never come. My honest prayer was, "God, grip my heart. I never want to doubt you or be unfaithful to my husband again."

God gave me a promise and a vision for my future that night through the words of Jeremiah 29:11: "For I know the plans I have for you," declares the Lord, "plans to prosper you and not to harm you, plans to give you hope and a future." (NIV)

The next morning was a Sunday. As Vaughan was getting ready to go to church, I asked if I could come along. I was not ready to tell him what I had just experienced; but I was just praying and hoping this time it was real. As I was getting ready and looking into the mirror, I was so excited. I felt as though I was getting ready to meet Jesus. For the first time in a very long time I had hope.

During the service I was reliving the dream I had the night before and praying, "God, please help me. Grip my heart and fill it with Your love. I want my relationship with You to be more than just a Sunday ritual. I need to feel Your presence. I need to know that You can give me the strength to overcome the sin that is in my life and not live in bondage to it. I desperately want a freedom that I have not felt for a very long time. I don't want to hold onto this pain as an excuse to keep you away any longer"

The musicians started to play worship music, yet I still couldn't feel my connection with God. I thought, "Could God really take away the sin that I felt was so much a part of me, like the freckles on my skin?" So, I just continued to pray. I listened as the pastor talked about God and how He can take my sins and help me in my walk with Him. I began to feel God tugging at my heart. For the first time in a very long time, I knew it was God answering my prayer to feel His presence and be free.

As the next song began to play, I remembered it from Bible College. This song had always touched my heart. I began to sing, "As the deer panteth for the water, so my soul longeth after Thee. You, alone are my heart's desire, and I long to worship Thee[5]." The tears began to fall and I was so thankful to be feeling God's presence again. I broke down inside and told Him how unworthy I had felt. I just allowed God to pour into my heart. As I did, He began to take my pain and give me peace and hope. It was like a cold glass of water on a hot summer's day. This was something I had longed for and needed so desperately.

After the service Vaughan was excited that I had really experienced God. I shared with him the dream I had had the night before and all that I had felt afterwards. He was very

---

5 "As the Deer" by Martin J. Nystrom, Written in 1981, based on Psalm 42:1;   https://en.wikipedia.org/wiki/As_the_Deer

encouraged. For the first time in a very long time we prayed together and then continued to talk for another couple hours. God was definitely working in both our lives. What seemed like an eternity away only a few days before, was now right in front of me. I could see a real future with God. I now had hope that my relationship with Him was being restored.

I was starting to feel great, but it wasn't long before the enemy was trying to make me doubt my experience with God. I was still struggling with some addictions and habits that I had made a part of my life. I knew this was not going to be an easy road and that these blockages would not just disappear on their own. I had many tough choices ahead of me. But God reassured me of that promise of 1 John 4:4 (KJV) that greater is He who is in me than he who is in the world. I knew that in my own strength I would definitely fail; but, with God on my side, I knew that I would get through this.

One of the areas I had struggled with was feeling loved. I knew Vaughan loved me but that just didn't seem like enough. Without God in my life, I had searched for attention in many different avenues. I knew that if God didn't replace it with something, I would find my own things to fill the void. One of the ways I had attempted to fill this void, was by going out with friends to the bars for drinks. I had also developed more unhealthy relationships on Facebook, and I was constantly pushing the boundaries. I knew that needed to change. I began deleting a bunch of people from my Facebook. This was the first step that would lead me one day to the other side of this pain. It was a slow, painful process, but I had to cut all communication with people that I felt would pose a threat to my restoration.

I was previously always fearful of Vaughan seeing my phone because I was afraid that he would see some of my messages. Even after I had cut all ties with any questionable relationships in my life, I still felt some fear. Would I pass the test and earn Vaughan's trust? Would I be strong enough to resist? I gave him full access to my accounts and my phone at any time to ensure accountability. This gave me a chance to be even more transparent with Vaughan. This allowed us to share in the victories we were overcoming together. It was getting easier.

I remember one time about 4 months after we established this new accountability, Vaughan and I had a mix up with our phone plans. For some reason he was receiving all my emails and texts and vice versa. I couldn't believe that for the first time I wasn't fearful. This time was different; I had God's help. I believe that phone mix up was the start of the realization that I was able to overcome the hold that sin had in my life. For the first time I had a clear conscience and was no longer afraid of Vaughan seeing something. I no longer had a secret life that I was trying to live. God was replacing my appetite for the forbidden with a loving relationship of fulfillment with Him and with Vaughan. I desired a right relationship with God, but, in order to have that, I had to let go of anything that was a danger to my marriage.

I truly felt excitement. Yet, what an uncomfortable statement to have to make to my husband, "I'm so glad I have nothing to hide!" I said to Vaughan, "Sweetie, I cannot promise you that I will never get another message that would be displeasing to you, but I can promise that I will be honest and provide you full disclosure to all my communications." He said, "Vahen, I love you and I trust you." My heart skipped a beat and I began to cry. I will never forget the healing I felt in my heart that day as I heard those words. It was in that moment I realized that we were going to make it. I came to understand that although I thought I could go through life on my own, a life without God would be empty and meaningless. I thank God every day for showing me His unconditional love and forgiveness through Vaughan.

I was able to allow God to heal my heart and I was able to forgive myself. I started to feel worthy of love again. Vaughan was seeing the transformation in my life and that helped us rebuild our love. The words "I love you" mean more now than I ever thought possible. We didn't see it at the time, but we would come to see how God is even able to take the pain we had experienced and use us to help others.

God offered us a fresh start and a real relationship with Him that is totally honest and transparent. His unconditional love gave us the courage to continue on. We began living this "fresh start" not in our own strength but in His. Vaughan and I grew to openly communicate our feelings without judgment. We were not afraid to ask the tough questions. We found out the hard way that it's the little things that affected us. If hidden or repressed, these "little things" would eventually create a chasm that will seem impossible to bridge. We learned that you can't build a relationship on lies or hidden secrets. Being transparent and open with each other was the only way we were able to start the healing process and move forward. Our greatest treasure emerging out of that season of God's gracious intervention in our lives was that our marriage was stronger and that we were more in love than the day we said, "I do."

Chapter 12

I Can Have Both?

Recommitting my life to God and feeling His love again brought just the most amazing feeling ever. I was actually starting to think that maybe I can still do something great for God. However, I didn't want to focus on a healing more than my relationship with God. I prayed, "Lord, I don't care about my healing. I just want you to grip my heart and I never want to doubt you again." My only desire was to be content with God and who I was in Him.

While I was rebuilding my relationship with the Lord, I was also grateful for the amazing friends He brought into my life to encourage me. I was especially thankful for the friend who had prayed with me about being healed "inside and out" just before I recommitted my life to the Lord. A couple weeks later she invited me to attend a weekend conference with her. A weekend away to focus on God was just what I needed. I didn't really know what to expect, but I went with a willingness to have God renew my heart and mind.

While I was worshiping God and feeling His presence again, I felt strength in my body that otherwise was not there. I actually got the desire to try and make steps and walk. I really thought that was crazy. I had just prayed to God and told Him I didn't care about a healing, so this must just be all in my head. Plus, what will people think? While I was standing and worshiping, the pastor of the church who was hosting this conference approached me and asked me if I wanted to take some steps. My response was, "I am able to walk a little and don't want people to think it's a miracle." The pastor said, "You just do what you can and God will do the rest."

I began walking across the front of the church with about 70 or 80 people following and praying. As I walked, I was very aware that some of the steps were especially difficult and awkward. I thought I was going to give up. It was hard not to focus on what the people might be thinking as they saw me, but I kept going. When I got back to my chair I didn't want to sit down just yet. I felt strength in my body that I had not felt before, so I remained standing. I knew that in my own strength this was not possible. Yes, I could stand and take a few steps with help, but I certainly could not walk all the way across the front of the church and back and then remain standing after that exertion. It really was God's strength in me. I had never experienced anything like this before. I mean it was really amazing, but I did not want to get caught up in the "hype" of something that was not of God. So, I began to pray and ask God to protect me and teach me to discern what is true. But how could I deny that this was anything other than God's power working in my body? I knew I couldn't walk across the front of the church like that and still have the strength to stay standing. It truly was God.

As my friend and I were talking about some of the amazing things that God had just done, a man I had never met before came over to me and said, "As I was praying for you, God showed me a Lego set. He showed me that He was putting you back together emotionally, spiritually, and physically. He was building a platform for you to shine. You are not forgotten. You have an anointed part to play. This is a new season for you. Speak the outcomes you want. God will hear and He will answer. He will come in power. God wants you to seek Him. The Spirit of the Lord has been sent to teach you all things." This was such an amazing, faith-giving word to receive from a total stranger!

As I was praying in my room that night, the Lord impressed an unusual phrase on my heart, "You can have both." I didn't really know at first what that was supposed to mean for me now. I was reminded of that time when I was five and God taught me the lesson that I could have both. As a child I had selected receiving a Bible over getting a $5.00 bill. The children's pastor had then handed me the Bible with another $5.00 bill inside. God was teaching me way back then that He wanted me to believe I could have both. Yes, I had reflected on that memory many times but didn't understand how it applied to my life as an adult. However, for some reason, now I could not help but see God's healing power and see how He was confirming to me, "I want you to have both."

So I prayed, "God, do you really want to heal me?" And the words the pastor said to me at the conference really came alive in my heart. "Vahen, when you're ready, you do what you can and God will do the rest!" That was so powerful because I was not even doing "what I can." I was afraid to work out or exercise because I was afraid that I would start to hope for something that would never happen. I didn't realize it at the time, but, looking back now, I believe that was when the Lord started showing me that I didn't have to be afraid. I could actually ask for big things from a big God. In reality, I hadn't even been doing spiritually "what I could." I was just hoping He would do it all. He was truly helping me understand the verse in Matthew 6:33. "But seek first the kingdom of God and His righteousness, and all these things shall be added to you."

From the very opening of the conference God was showing me that I truly *can* have a deeper relationship with Him—a relationship that I did not think was possible after all of the mistakes I had made.

The next day one of the speakers at the conference approached me and said, "I have a word for this lady and I want to pray for her." She said, "There is so much hunger inside of you. God says 'blessed are those who hunger and thirst after righteousness for they will be filled'. The Lord has seen your hunger and that hunger is drawing His presence to you. The Lord wants you to know that there are no limitations for you in the Spirit; you are going to be able to do things for the globe. God is going to give you visions for different countries and different nations. Maybe you'll actually go there, I don't know, but I feel you are going to start here from this place. You're going to do things that are going to help other nations and other people--especially the poor. God has given you a heart with great compassion."

She continued by saying, "Last night I noticed you had the most beautiful pair of boots and now you have on another pair of beautiful boots. As soon as I saw those boots, God reminded me of an old song, 'These boots are made for walking, and that's just what they'll do; one of these days these boots are gonna walk all over you.' I feel like the Lord said that in the Spirit you are going to walk all over the devil with the ministry that God has put into your heart."

She paused and asked me if this was making sense. I was speechless at first, but then said, "You don't know the half of it!" I knew what was deep in my heart. I knew I had a strong desire for God and that I wanted to have an impact on the world for Him, but how did she know? God was giving her this prophetic word for me because He wanted me to know that He was with me and that I could still reach my dreams.

Then she continued to pray a prophetic prayer for me, "Lord, You just want to bless this woman. You want her to know that You are strongly attracted to her hunger and that You are with her even in her house. You see her worshiping in her house. You see her lying on her bed. Like the Psalms say, 'I commune with the Lord on my bed at night.' I just see God with you while you are awake, just before you drift off to sleep. I see you communing with the Lord. And this great intimacy with God will bring great fruitfulness to you, in Jesus Name."

Talk about having God speak into your life! Even though I was hearing all this, I was still thinking: "I don't know how to trust what is being said. I need to put this aside and continue to pray and ask God for wisdom." I was hopeful that God did want me to fulfill my dreams and perhaps He did want to heal me, but I just wanted to focus on Him healing my heart. I think it's funny that amidst all my efforts to maintain my focus on God and not on healing, God was slowly building my faith. And, my faith was increasing even more as I drew closer to Him.

Even after all that, the enemy was immediately at work to convince me that I had not really heard from God. Deep in my heart I felt that this was the desire of God for me. However, I dared not tell anyone because they would think I was crazy— unstable even. This would be just like that nurse in the hospital who thought I needed psychiatric attention when I spoke about walking down the aisle on my wedding day. Afraid of being wrong or being let down by God, I decided to play it safe with my Christian walk. I would privately believe that God has the power to heal and do amazing things, but I would not tell anyone that I believed He wanted to do it for me.

I began to feel uncertain and thought, "But I don't want to start holding back from God. If God was wanting to bless me, how could I hold back telling others about it? How do I move forward with this new vision?" Before I had the chance to verbalize this to anyone, a pastor I knew came up and declared a prayer over me: "I rebuke that fear and doubt that the enemy is trying to place upon you, Vahen. God wants you to know that He is pleased with your faith in Him. The enemy has no authority over the power of God. Vahen, this is your time and God wants to bless you."

I can hardly believe all the words that had been spoken into my life at that weekend conference. Apparently God was really wanting to confirm to me that He was the One speaking to me and it was not just all in my head. Yet another gentleman whom I did not know approached me with these words: "Satan will try to come against what God has already done in your spirit and your body. But God wants you to do what you can." He continued to repeat the very words I had heard before. He advised me that I should pray daily about my healing and continue doing what I *can* and God will do the rest. I could not believe my ears, as this was the same message that the other gentleman had just given me. He finished the conversation by telling me to remember two scriptures: Romans 4:17 "…'I have made you a father of many nations'" in the presence of Him whom he believed—God, who gives life to the dead and calls those things which do not exist as though they did." Ezekiel 37 was the second scripture. That chapter is all about a valley of dry bones where the Lord told Ezekiel to prophesy to the dry bones for them to live.

The Lord was really confirming His plan to me. He was making it very plain that I needed to "walk in His word" so I could believe and not doubt His voice. God does want to heal me and restore me to complete health. But I knew that it wasn't because I wanted to walk the beach or play volleyball again. (Even though that would be an added bonus, that's not what my heart desired). I knew it was because He wanted to heal me to bring honor and glory to Him. I felt such peace in my heart as I said, "God, thank you for healing me!" Would I feel that same peace every day? No, I guarantee I will not. But from that point I had a renewed expectation and looked forward to what God would do next. "Now faith is the substance of things hoped for, the evidence of things not seen." Hebrews 11:1 (KJV)

After this revelation, I felt strongly that I no longer had to look for validation through "man." I knew God would continue to speak to me. I could trust in what God had promised me. Although I still didn't know when my promise would be fulfilled, I prayed that I would stay the course. I was confident that God was leading me. That's all the validation I needed. I made a vow to be faithful to do the things God asked of me, because He knows best, and I knew He would protect me.

♡Chapter 13

A Dream Restored

Many years ago my father-in-law ("Father John" as he likes to be called) introduced me to a book entitled *The Dream Giver* by Bruce Wilkinson[6]. It's about a man called Ordinary who is living in the land of familiar and doing what every other anybody was doing[7]. Stepping out to reach his dream, Ordinary was faced with many obstacles; but, he kept pushing forward and ultimately reached his dream[8]. When I first read it I saw myself in Ordinary. I thought of all the physical, marital, and spiritual obstacles I had faced. These obstacles had caused me to conclude that my dream was unachievable. Reading that book made me realize that although I did have many obstacles, so do many other people. I just need to keep pushing forward to reach my dream.

The next time I saw Father John I just had to thank him for the influence he had on my life. I talked about how his encouragement and support had really helped me. I told him that I believed God was taking my fear and replacing it with

6 Bruce Wilkinson, The Dream Giver: Following your God-Given Destiny (Multnomah Books, 2003)

7 Bruce Wilkinson, The Dream Giver: Following your God-Given Destiny (Multnomah Books, 2003) p.7

8 Bruce Wilkinson, The Dream Giver: Following your God-Given Destiny (Multnomah Books, 2003) p.8

courage and boldness. Some of that was because of the way he would challenge me to think outside the box and to look at God in the everyday things. Also, I felt that God was using this time to teach me to wait as He provides more opportunities.

Sitting at the table that day was really a special time as we swapped stories about the things God has done in our lives. I felt my stories paled in comparison to his ministry working with Wycliffe Bible Translators and visiting over sixty-two countries. I could have listened for hours about his adventures, but one thing he shared really stayed in my heart.

He told me that everywhere he went, people would ask him to share my story: the story about my illness and yet marrying his son. He said everywhere he would go people would ask, "Can you tell us that story about your daughter-in-law again?" or "We heard about your son and his wife in the wheelchair; can you please tell us that story?"

On one of his travels to Africa a man approached him and asked, "How could you allow that to happen?" Not being exactly sure what he meant, Father John responded. "What do you mean?" The man replied, "How could you allow your son to marry a "broken" girl?" From his perspective, Father John had let his son and family down by bringing a disabled person into it. In their culture a disabled person was a burden and a detriment to the entire family. It was actually humorous because my father-in-law knew that although I may be in a wheelchair, I was far from broken! He had an opportunity to share more of my testimony with this man.

Father John was always one who liked to challenge people and encourage them to think outside the box. That day as we were talking I don't know if he realized just how serious I was about my teenage dream of going to Africa. However, he saw an opportunity that was just too tempting to pass up. He asked me. "So, what would it take to get you to go to Africa and tell your story yourself?"

I was eager to discuss this possibility with Vaughan who was amazed that I was even considering such a challenge. I told him what his father had shared. I endeavored to tell him that although it was truly a spontaneous and surprising plan, I actually felt faith rise up within me. Knowing that Vaughan would not only want to protect me from challenges and inconvenience, would he even be open to such a trip? As we talked together I could see the Lord giving Vaughan the faith and the assurance that this really was of God.

I didn't even know how this trip could be possible. I knew that it would take a toll on me both physically and emotionally, but we began the planning process anyway. Knowing that I could not possibly do this in my own strength, I reached out for prayer support. I knew that having a team of people praying for me would be key to accomplish the dream which had just become a God-assignment. My home church (Evangel Pentecostal Assembly), my parents' church in Newfoundland, and many others came alongside Vaughan and I. We not only received prayer support, but also received financial blessings to make it possible. We were not expecting this kind of partnership, but we were very grateful.

The closer the date came, the more I began having some anxiety and doubts about what I was doing. I couldn't get my focus off all the barriers and challenges that I was going to face. I began to wonder if this whole trip was just my idea or was it really what God wanted for me? Yes, I was having serious doubts.

I felt that if I didn't have so many obstacles to overcome, maybe then it would be possible for me to fulfill God's purpose in my life. Turning to my devotional as I often did when I needed answers or support, I saw the title for my daily reading. I couldn't believe my eyes as I read the title: "Influence - Uniquely You." The daily reading began: "Have you thought about all the events that have led to this point? Why you are here? And what caused you to seek God or read this devotional? I believe He knew exactly where you would be right now and what you would need. He knew about your passions and gifts and the platform you would have. I believe God is very purposeful in designing your life. He made you to be uniquely significant, and to have an eternal impact on the world around you[9]."

Once again I was hearing His voice! As I read it, such a weight lifted. God was reminding me that I am exactly where He wants me and that He would protect me. I felt more courage and I even wondered if maybe God would heal me before I went to Africa. Even if the healing did not mean that I was necessarily walking on my own, yet it would be wonderful to be healed from the other major health issues I had.

On many occasions I have thought about that prayer I received in college. The president had prayed that God would bless my ministry and strengthen my whole body, even my digestive system. That prayer would often encourage me as I realized that God knew even then what I would struggle with and He would one day heal me. However, there were times that I thought maybe it was just to show me that He was going to give me the strength to endure it. You see, the health issues that I struggled with controlled my life and my schedule. I always had to make sure I knew where the bathroom was. On any given day, I would need to have up to 5 hours of private time for my bathroom routine. I thought, "How can I go to Africa and stay at someone's home and explain why I would need to

---

9 "Influence - Uniquely You." by Tony Dungy; "The Uncommon Life
   Daily Challenge"

lock myself in the bathroom for part of the day." There were times when even after three or more hours in the bathroom I would leave with no success. It was frustrating to know that I just wasted 3 hours of my time with nothing to show for it. It felt like I was a prisoner without any control over my life. Feeling bloated and uncomfortable was a feeling I had somehow learned to cope with; but, my biggest challenge was the emotional battle of having to find the strength to go about my day. I would also be left questioning why God wouldn't heal my body.

Many times I felt abandoned by God and alone in my pain. This was especially real one night before going to Africa. I cried out, "God, where are You? I know You see me! I know You feel my pain! Why is this not better yet? I just don't understand!" It was in such moments as these that I would bargain with God and say: "God, I don't care about being in this wheelchair, but please just heal my digestive system. I can't go to Africa in this situation."

The next morning after the painful and emotional night in the bathroom, I felt I wanted to start my day right. I again turned to read my daily devotional entitled "All My Tears." The scripture for the day was Psalm 56:8. "You keep track of all my sorrows. You have collected all my tears in your bottle. You have recorded each one in your book." (NLT) As tears welled up in my eyes, I continued to read: "It is a common misconception, if God doesn't rescue us from our pain, then He must not know we are suffering. In actuality this verse tells us how much God feels our pain. He records each and every pain we feel! Can you imagine how big His book must be on our lives? When we experience worries and pain, God is validating them. God knows your problems and sees your tears. Take heart in knowing

God is personal with you and hears the pain in your voice[10]."

Once again God gave me peace. I know the Lord truly does give me the strength for my day and joy in my heart. Even as I battled with health issues, I chose to trust in His promises. Hebrews 13:5 says, "God will never leave you nor forsake you." More than that, I gained a new certainty; I knew I had hope. I do have a future. I will prosper and I will be healed. Hebrews 11:1 states that "Now faith is the substance of things hoped for, and the evidence of things not seen." Preparation for Africa became a time for me to learn valuable lessons about pushing beyond what I physically felt like or how things looked. It was becoming more and more possible to hope and trust in God's promise.

Yet, it was not easy to exercise miracle-believing faith in my situation. Any disruptions to my eating and bathroom routines would cause me to suffer for days or sometimes weeks without relief; and, now I'm planning on going to Africa? I would be running the risk of experiencing any and all of this in a third world country where half the bathrooms are holes in the ground and the menu is unknown to me. How would I even get around in my chair without modern sidewalks? What was I thinking?

I can't comprehend how, but God calmed my fears once again by His truth in Matthew 19:26. He reminded me that "With man this is impossible, but with God all things are possible."

Many times I had wondered if I'd ever have a platform from which to share. Now, with all our plans in place and tickets in hand, we boarded the plane to Africa that first week of May, 2012. Who would have thought that I would actually roll onto that long-desired platform in a wheelchair!

---

10 "All My Tears." by Tony Dungy; "The Uncommon Life Daily Challenge"

♡Chapter 14

A Life-Changing Journey

It was a long journey from my high school graduation when it was announced that my dream was to be a missionary in Africa, to the day I actually arrived in Entebbe, Uganda. I am so excited to share with you this life-changing experience that I never thought would happen.

My father-in-law, "Father John" as he is affectionately known, took the lead on planning the trip. Through his work with Wycliffe Bible Translators, he was familiar with the area. He arranged speaking engagements and various meetings over the duration of the two weeks we would spend in Africa. Our schedule for the first week was to speak at local churches, small groups, and the African Bible University in Entebbe. In our second week Vaughan and I would help facilitate a Leadership Matters training course with Father John and a few other trained pastors.

The Leadership Matters course provides practical ministry training and skill development related to ministry. The course headings illustrate the variety in the program: Motivation, Life Planning, Management, Public Relations, Communication, Creative Thinking, Decision-Making, and Building Relationships[11].

---

11 www.lmccourse.org

When Vaughan and I were first married we had the opportunity to take this training in Holland. We saw it as an invaluable tool for ministry training. Soon we would be on location in a little village just a few hours outside the city of Entebbe. Leaders from all over Africa were coming to take part and we would have the amazing opportunity to assist as facilitators.

After a very long flight we finally touched down on African soil. All the preparation and planning in the world could not have prepared me for the rollercoaster of emotions of that first day. Yes, the journey was long and tiresome, but the excitement of being there was just the most amazing feeling ever. As we approached the arrivals waiting area, my heart pounded. I had the biggest ear-to-ear smile ever. I was finally here and about to greet my new African friends. The pastor of the orphanage where we would stay for the first week was there to meet us, plus another pastor who would be helping facilitate the Leadership course. Among that welcoming party was also our translator and friend whom I had met previously when she came to Canada with Father John. What a grand reception. I knew we were going to get a warm welcome, but I didn't expect to have our own welcoming party gathered at the airport awaiting our arrival. Yes, I was exhausted, but somehow I didn't even think about that. They were so excited to meet us and I wanted them all to feel my genuine appreciation.

We stepped outside of the airport and got into our separate cars. It was truly amazing to see how they packed all our luggage and my chair in such a compact vehicle. As we were driving away in the pouring rain, my eyes were fixated on the scenery around me. I don't really know what I was expecting, but poverty was definitely evident. What I saw as broken-down shacks were actually people's homes. My emotions went from feelings of excitement to heart-wrenching sadness. I thought,

"Dear God, what do I have to offer these people? Why am I here?" I began to mentally prepare myself for the days and weeks ahead. Silently I prayed, "God, show me my purpose here and give me Your strength."

We were offered hospitality by a local pastor with his wonderful family. He had graciously come to the airport to welcome us. In addition to their church responsibilities, he and his wife also ran an orphanage of 22 children. Everyone was so happy that we were coming. The pastor's wife, their family, and all the children in the orphanage were just so excited for our arrival to their home. Like many in the various places we visited, they could not wait to meet us and hear us share. I thought, "Wow, what an honour!" However, I still didn't understand why I was worthy of such recognition.

On our first night, our hosts had arranged a meet and greet in their home, where we had the opportunity to get to know some people in a more intimate setting. As we were sitting around chatting a bit and waiting for everyone to arrive, I was introduced to my interpreter. Whoa! It had completely slipped my mind that some of the people coming might not even speak English. Now I was getting nervous. I had never done this "interpreting stuff" before!

As I was collecting my thoughts, Father John turned to me and said, "So, Vahen, did you know you've already made an impact here?" My reaction was, "What do you mean? I just got here, and I haven't even spoken yet." He told me that one of the pastors who had just met us at the airport was so overwhelmed by my cheerfulness and bubbly disposition that he couldn't stop talking about it during the drive from the airport. He couldn't understand how I was so happy. "What is this that I am seeing? How is this person in a wheelchair filled with such joy?"

When I heard this I was really encouraged. I knew God was showing me my purpose for coming to Africa and my doubts and fears began to subside. This also helped calm my nerves about speaking with an interpreter for the first time. I was glad that I had good notes because having to speak in short phrases made it easy to lose my train of thought. However, for this small-town Newfoundland girl who tends to talk fast normally, it wasn't quite as scary as I thought. As I spoke I could see their faces receiving and processing my story. Even though we spoke a different language and lived continents apart, I realized that the message of hope and God's strength and help transcends all language or cultural barriers.

You can never really know the impact you will make in someone's life, whether it is through a one-time meeting or a daily interaction. The more I learned about these people and their culture, the more I started to see how much I had to offer by way of encouragement—not because of what I have accomplished, but because of the God-given joy and strength I have, in spite of adversity. That first night after I shared our story, a lady who had been afflicted with an auto-immune disorder said to me, "I just had to come meet you. I have heard your story from your father-in-law, but I needed to see for myself. I wanted to see your smile and see God's strength in you. You are such an encouragement to me. Can you please pray with me?"

A few days later, I was scheduled to speak at the African Bible University. When we arrived the president was very accommodating and apologized for the lack of accessibility. I responded, "Don't worry. I'm okay. I have Vaughan and Father John to lift my chair and carry me around. I can go anywhere." I think that made him feel at ease as we all shared a chuckle.

There were about 100 students and 5 professors sitting in the chapel as I shared my story. These represented the "called ones" of this region. The male students were dressed in dress shirts and ties and outnumbered the ladies in their colourful dresses. They were accustomed to an academic environment, so what were they expecting to hear from this wheelchair?

Undistracted by the fear of being open and vulnerable, I shared how I went through a period of my life when I pretended that things were better than they were. I did this because I feared I would be judged. I also told them how I needed them to see that we all need to turn to God for strength no matter who we are or what struggle we might be facing. I emphasized that we need to keep our focus on God or we will get distracted and even fail.

Afterwards, the president came to me, and said, "Amazing! I could not do what you just did—the way you shared with such vulnerability and transparency. This is what people really need to see, but not everyone can do that. This message is so relevant to what the Ugandan people are feeling. So I thank you." What a contrast to the lies and fears that had so often plagued me. Why had I wasted so much time thinking that "perfection" (for which I was no longer eligible) was the loudest testimony, when all the time God just wanted me to have total dependency on Him?

I heard so many encouraging words that day at the University. Another man told me, "We really needed to hear the things you shared today. You are a genuine person. When you smile, it reaches inside people. We can see that you are truly happy in your circumstances and that is so encouraging for us to see."

Time after time as we worked our way through the two-week schedule I experienced God's peace and strength. I proved just how real it is that He was able to help me overcome all my personal challenges faced on the trip and do what He had called me to do. I believe that discovery was more of an encouragement to me than I can even begin to express.

Another amazing experience during that first week was the opportunity to connect with all the orphans our host pastor and his family cared for. We were given a tour of the small building beside their home that the 22 orphans shared. They were very well behaved and everyone helped out. They shared everything from washing the laundry by hand, feeding the chickens, making meals, or doing other chores around the house. We even had 4 or 5 volunteers wash my wheelchair from top to bottom after I got it muddy trying to get a tour of the property. These children had been shown love and given a place to call home by a family without a lot of money, but just a big heart.

One of my favorite memories of the children was when they all got together and sang and danced for us. I could have listened to them all night. I was just so captivated by how the sound of their voices just pierced my soul. They were some of the most joyful children I had ever seen. With tears rolling down my face, I thought to myself, "I don't think I have ever witnessed a more beautiful moment."

As a person with a disability, I have faced and regularly overcome many challenges. These unique challenges include everything from how I managed my daily routine to how people viewed me. Yet, compared to other parts of the developing world, our home country of Canada has made significant progress with eliminating many mobility and accessibility challenges. It seems like there was already someone forging ahead and blazing a trail for you in North America, and finding a way to assist with many of the tough challenges I'd usually face.

My decision to travel to Africa was one of the biggest mobility challenges I had ever willingly subjected myself to. This time I was to be the trailblazer. With the hopes of giving me a better understanding of what to prepare for, I was warned about the "roads." I was told that the potholes were more like pits and I would require a road map to navigate out of them. One would think this was the last place a person in my situation should be. In preparation, we had purchased a specialized fifth wheel for my wheelchair. It was designed to be attached to the front of my wheelchair to give it greater stability on rough terrain. I thought I was good to go.

Vaughan was amazing throughout the whole trip. Without him this adventure wouldn't have been the same. We discovered on one of our first days out, our planning wasn't as foolproof as we hoped. Vaughan, eager to see what this fifth wheel was capable of, said, "Let's take it for a test run down the driveway." I looked down the "driveway" filled with those deep ruts. With slight tremor of fear in my voice, I disagreed, "Vaughan, I won't make it." I could see how excited he was to have me put this fifth wheel to the test. With bold confidence, he encouraged me by saying, "Don't worry, you'll be fine! You have the *FIFTH WHEEL!*" I should have been a bit quicker and suggested he volunteer for this adventure, but instead I took a deep breath and gingerly began to navigate down the lane. I can't remember if it took 30 seconds or a minute from the time I heard, "Don't worry, you'll be fine," until the moment where I started to tip past the point of no return. "Vaughan, help!" I yelled, and over I went. Falling sideways out of my chair into the red dirt, I looked up and cried out "What was that you were saying?"

You should have seen the faces of the onlookers. Even though Vaughan had been close, he wasn't fast enough to stop me from capsizing. He was leaning over me apologizing profusely. When he saw that I was laughing so hard I couldn't move, we all just burst into laughter. Thankfully we had it all recorded on camera, so I turned around and gave a big thumbs up to the viewers. As I mentioned earlier, without Vaughan this adventure wouldn't have been the same!

Like a trooper, I went out to the craft shops in the nearby village. The extra wheel helped me there for sure, but it was the bumpiest shopping experience I ever had. Most of the time the shops were too narrow and I couldn't get in between the merchandise. I found myself outside pointing in at things that I wanted to be brought out to me so I could take a closer look. However, like the true shopper I am, I was successful in finding a few souvenirs to bring home, including a colourful African dress.

Even though most of this country seemed to be built around stairs and ruts, surprisingly I did find some accessible facilities in the bigger city nearby. It was not to the standards we have in Canada, but there were actually a few malls and shopping areas that had ramps and bigger bathroom stalls. One thing I learned quite quickly was to keep hand sanitizer and some form of toilet paper with me at all times.

Whether I was navigating impossible roads or getting myself

in and out of the mosquito net during the night, each mobility challenge was overcome. When we first met, I had called Vaughan my "knight in shining armour." More than once on the trip he was put to the test. His "rescues" also included being my human elevator!

And, of course, there was no end to cultural differences that caught our attention. As we were travelling with our local pastor friend, Vaughan saw him using three different cell phones. Intrigued, Vaughan asked him why he had so many cell phones. The pastor explained that the cell phone companies offered free calling plans in different areas. So, he would use each free phone when he was in the appropriate free areas. We discovered many intriguing (and creative) practices!

From the very onset of this trip we experienced warmth and hospitality everywhere we went. We often felt like royalty. Everyone we met was so excited to sit and talk with us. They hung onto our every word. They were so happy that we came all the way from Canada to visit with them.

We received wonderful feedback from our times of ministry. I would like to acknowledge that my husband Vaughan's support was invaluable. If it were not for him, I don't know if I would even have a story to share. However, I think it was in Africa that I first felt that I could see how God would use us to speak together as a couple. I just needed to pray about that since Vaughan would always say, "I support you, honey, but the spotlight is for you not me." Deep down, I knew that God would work that out in His time.

Surprisingly, this opportunity came in our second week at the Leadership Matters training camp. Vaughan was asked if he would share his thoughts right after I shared my testimony. It was an amazing moment for me. Yes, I had received his love and forgiveness, but to hear him share from his heart to others meant the world to me. When we were finished, a twenty-year-old man said to Vaughan, "In a culture like ours where a man can have several wives, most men would quickly move on and choose another woman. This story of your courage is one I will never forget. You truly are a man of great strength." He then turned to me and said, "And when can I read your book?" At that point I had no idea I was even going to write a book, but I feel that his comment planted a seed that started taking root in my heart. This time I knew it was a "good seed." God was really showing me glimpses into my future. He was restoring not only my marriage, but my dreams to make a difference in the world. It seemed everywhere we went while in Uganda, the common questions were, "When will you be back?" and, "When can we read your book?"

It was on our final Sunday morning in Africa that the Lord gave me one of the most significant experiences or discoveries of the whole trip. The pastor held a Bible study before the morning service. As Vaughan and I were sitting in the chapel listening to the pastor, he asked the congregation: "Do we believe God answers all our prayers?" Some of the people replied "Yes", but another said, "Sometimes the answer is 'no' or 'wait.'" Then the pastor turned and looked at me and said, "God has just answered Vahen's prayer today. When Vahen was a teenager in high school she prayed that she would be a missionary in Africa and now today she is finally here! This shows us that there is no expiration date on prayer. Never give up hope or stop praying."

Although I had recalled that prayer many times, in that moment the reality of it really sank into my heart. Yes, God did hear my prayer about going to Africa. He did hear my prayer about making an impact on the world. He showed me that everything I had gone through so far had led me to this point. I could not have made the impact that I did had I not been able to show joy through hardship. It was in that moment that I truly understood James 1:2-4, "Consider it all joy, my brethren, when you encounter various trials, knowing that the testing of your faith produces endurance. And let endurance have its perfect result, so that you may be perfect and complete, lacking in nothing."

I had really hoped and prayed that God would heal me before I went to Africa. Instead, God gave me the strength to reach my dreams in spite of my circumstance. I accomplished my dream because I allowed God to use me *in* my circumstance. It was as if a light bulb went on in my head and I said, "I understand now, God." As difficult as some of the journey was on me physically, I was constantly reassured that I was exactly where I was supposed to be.

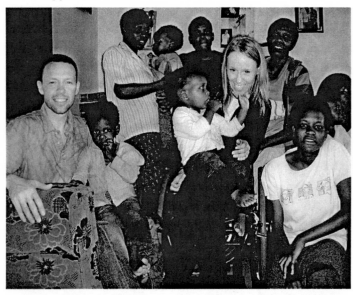

During the long flight home Vaughan and I reflected on the many different experiences of our two weeks. We concluded that despite the very real physical challenges I had to face, I had seen how God could use me as He gave me such settled peace in the midst of circumstances and inconveniences. I definitely experienced "the peace of God, which surpasses all understanding." Philippians 4:7. God blessed me with this amazing opportunity to make a difference. I knew that I would never view my struggles in the same way again. There were countless reminders that I can always trust God no matter what comes my way. This life-changing journey set my expectation on what else God has for me. My hope is that my steps of faith will encourage others not to give up on their dreams.

Chapter 15

Expanded Influence

Not long after returning from Africa, I started getting more invitations to speak. I had been praying for ministry opportunities and now God was opening doors. People were interested in hearing about my most recent adventure and I was even invited back to Newfoundland on two separate occasions to speak. In this new season of expanded influence, He was teaching me major principles and life disciplines for effectiveness in ministry.

It was truly incredible to see how God was using my experiences for His glory; yet I was still dealing with feelings of guilt and unworthiness from my past mistakes. I remember a conversation I had with my sister Erica before one of my speaking engagements in Newfoundland. I said, "Sis, you have seen me hit rock bottom, almost ruin my marriage, get angry at God, and now you're going to hear me speak about how great God is. I feel like such a hypocrite, and now I'm questioning myself." She looked at me and said, "Vahen, no one wants to hear from someone who has never been through some "stuff." You've made it through some tough times and now you are showing people it's really possible to overcome your failures." That really lifted my spirits! Her comments were so reminiscent of the words I heard from the president of the African Bible University in Africa. I vividly recalled how he had seen my vulnerability and transparency as a way to tell the story of God's empowering grace which flows into the "gap" of my dependency on Him. I started to see that sharing about the hurdles in my life would show people that there is AUTHENTIC hope. Oh how I was learning that "dependency" is BIG with God!

I was about to experience another important principle about expanded influence and effective ministry. I discovered in a very powerful way that dependency on God is expressed in obedience to follow His promptings. Aside from sharing my story that night, I also talked about how important it is to listen to God and to be obedient in what He is asking us to do. Because of my experience of doubting myself and not trusting God, I felt strongly to encourage others to listen to God's voice. It's so important that we learn to listen, because Isaiah 50:4 says, "The Lord GOD has given me the tongue of the learned, that I should know how to speak a word in season to him who is weary. He awakens me morning by morning, He awakens my ear to hear as the learned." You may think that hearing God's voice has to be a profound encounter where the heavens open up and you get an instant answer. However, from my experience, I have come to realize that He uses even the simplest of things to make a big impact. It's more about taking that first step in faith and being obedient in the little things. It may be as simple as feeling a tug on your heart to do or say something that might seem odd or unexplainable. Yet you feel that someone would really be blessed by your obedience.

Allow me to share another time when I had experienced this firsthand. We were having prayer time at a church in Newfoundland. I had the word *"salvation"* drop into my heart. I didn't know what I was going to do, but I just felt *"salvation."* I looked up and saw a man standing at the back of the room just observing. I thought that maybe I was being directed to talk to this person about salvation. Without being too obvious, I casually made my way back toward him, stopping to say, "Hi" to a couple other people. When I got to him, I introduced myself and told him that I was the daughter of Pastor Ings and I was visiting for a week. He told me that he and his wife attended this church and he was just waiting for her. After a brief chat with him I started to make my way back to the front. Admittedly I was feeling silly. It seemed that I was totally off the mark with what I thought God wanted me to do. That man didn't need salvation. I started to question if I had really heard God and I started to feel defeated.

As I was heading back to the front, I passed a lady that I felt drawn to talk with. I wheeled up beside her and put my arm on the back of the seat behind her and just started talking with her. She started telling me how discouraged she was and how she felt like God was so far away. She said, "I know you understand how I feel because of what you have been through." I just encouraged her and told her that God is actually right beside her and waiting for her to see that she can trust Him with anything.

In my mind I thought, "Here is a lady who has a relationship with Jesus, but she just needs some encouragement." We talked for a while and then I asked her if I could pray for her. To my surprise, she got up from her seat and went up to the front. The next thing I knew she was praying with my dad and accepting Jesus into her heart.

Later she told my mom that she had wanted to give her life to Jesus for a long time, but she was held back by hurt and fear. She continued to say, "If Vahen had not talked to me that night, I don't think I would have made that step because the next day I had a family crisis. Normally that would have just made me angry at God. Instead, I was able to ask God for His strength."

A few months later, when I was preparing to return for my second speaking engagement, my mother told me how excited this lady was to see me again. She wanted to give me a big hug and thank me again for being obedient to God and talking with her. I was feeling so blessed that God used me to bring someone to "salvation."

One week before I was to fly back to Newfoundland, I got a call from my mother telling me that this lady had passed away in her sleep. I began to weep as my mind flashed right back to that night when I felt that word *"salvation"* in my heart. "Dear God, thank you for prompting me and helping me listen to Your voice. It's because of things like this that I'm asking you, God, to please help me to always be faithful and listen to Your voice no matter how silly something sounds or how uncomfortable I may feel." I was really starting to understand what it meant to make an impact on the world around me for God. The joy that came from knowing a person made it into heaven because I was faithful was a feeling I never want to forget.

With expanded influence and an increase in ministry opportunities, I was also being challenged to find the necessary stamina. It was now time to return for that second trip to Newfoundland. It was months ago on the flight back from my first ministry trip to Newfoundland that I had told the Lord, "God, if this is what it takes to do this type of ministry, I can't keep this up." Previously, after each speaking engagement and another long day, I would leave feeling so physically and spiritually drained. I felt that I had just used up all my energy. With my physical condition, I didn't know how I would be able to do it all over again. I would so easily become discouraged. Yet I knew that God was using me in spite of my weakness. I knew the reason that I was drawn to fast and pray before this trip was because He knew I needed strength that I did not have in myself.

Before each trip I would pray, "God, you know how I struggle. Can you please heal me?" My dreams had become my reality, yet I didn't know how I could keep going. I didn't think I was mentally or physically strong enough. I needed to trust that God would give me what I needed for wherever He would lead me. It was then that I felt God say, "*YOU* can't do it! You can't do it without *Me!* You need to stay close to Me so I can give you the strength you need." I was feeling convicted that my little *warm fuzzy* devotional, with one scripture verse per day was just not enough. This became an area of my life that the Lord would revisit in the months ahead. However, I was beginning to see clearly that my dependency and stamina were all closely linked with that closer relationship with Him.

Not only was I feeling very blessed as invitations began to come for speaking engagements to share my life and experiences with other people, I was also pleased to begin to receive opportunities to write about it. These would ultimately lead me towards the writing of this book. On this journey I had many opportunities to measure how God was slowly building my strength in every area of my life.

My very first writing experience was about three years after I got sick with Transverse Myelitis. I was asked to write an article for *Good Tidings* - a magazine published by the Pentecostal Assemblies of Newfoundland and Labrador. I knew what I wanted to say but didn't really know how to write it so I worked with one of my professors from college. He wrote out the story from my perspective. Then many years later, I did a follow up article after Vaughan and I came through some tough marital challenges. I connected with their editor and she helped *me* write my own story. Over the years God continued to give me opportunities to develop my writing skills.

By the time I was asked to write about my Africa experience I was gaining more confidence as a writer. I was approached by Spinal Cord Injury Alberta, to write an ariticle in their *Spinal Columns* magazine. This gave me the opportunity to reach and inspire people with disabilities. God was allowing me to use my life to influence others and make a difference. I started to notice that living as a person with a disability also enhanced my ministry opportunities. I knew that regardless of my situation, I had true joy because of God in my life.

I began seeing how God was giving me even more opportunities to grow. I became involved in the ladies group at my church and eventually I was privileged to lead a group every Wednesday morning. This role gave me more accountability and kept me close to God. I came to realize that the waiting and the delays in the past that I saw as an inconvenience or that I had interpreted as God not caring, were actually Him ensuring that I would keep right on track and be in step with His perfect timing. He taught me that a waiting period is also a period of growth. I learned that waiting on God didn't mean I was sitting around while I waited for Him to open doors. No, waiting on God meant I was to seek Him and be faithful with whatever He gave me. I was feeling so blessed to have these opportunities. This only increased my desire for a deeper relationship with Him. After years of feeling unworthy and wondering if I would ever do anything for God, He was giving me peace and contentment. I could clearly see He was providing me a platform to share my experiences for His glory. He was preparing me, so I would be strong enough for the ministry He was leading me into. He was taking me farther than I ever thought possible.

♡Chapter 16

My Compass! My Guide!

I was entering unchartered territory. God was calling me into a deeper relationship with Him than I ever had before. As I became more intentional about my time with the Lord, He was teaching me to listen and to follow where He leads. Ministry in my own strength was exhausting. I also found I often struggled with taking on things that were not mine to take on. Whenever I would do that, I would get distracted and weighed down by burdens that weren't mine to carry. I soon realized that I needed to be careful about how I spent my time and who I allowed to speak into my life. I desired true intimacy with God more than an active social life. This realization was a harsh reality for this "social butterfly."

I remember reading this quote by Ruth Haley Barton in her book, *Strengthening the Soul of Your Leadership*. "The only way to begin facing these challenges is to keep seeking tenaciously after God through spiritual disciplines that keep us grounded in the presence of God at the corner of our being. Solitude and silence in particular enable us to experience a place of authenticity within and to invite God to meet us there. In that place of our seeking we listen for that still, small voice of God telling us who we really are and what is real from a spiritual point of view. Then we are not quite so enslaved by the demands and expectations of life in leadership[12]."

I felt validated in my choice to pull back in my social life. It really helped me understand my struggle as I sought to find a balance in my life's purpose.

God is so faithful in bringing people into your path or giving you insights at just the right time. I remember another time when I was talking to Father John and I asked him, "How do you tell someone that you need a break because they are taking up too much of your emotional brain space?" His response was so valuable to me. "Vahen, your greatest fulfillment will come through encouraging people to become all that God has created them to be. *However*, your biggest challenge in accomplishing that is to decrease some of the busy times when you'd rather be relating to people. In order to discover God at a deeper level and develop discernment, you have to carve out inordinate amounts of time to be alone with God. There will be some pain in embracing that balance, but it will be a choice of whether to reject intimacy with God or influence with people."

When I found myself in situations where I would take on more than what God had called me to, it was always harder to stay focused and have faith. It seemed that I was constantly asking God for confirmation because I kept losing my focus. I would pray, "God, I am sorry that I continue to doubt You. Please give me Your wisdom as I stay focused on the things You are already saying to me." I was beginning to understand the importance of setting my boundaries and staying close to Him.

I think it's really neat the way God uses situations to steer me back to where He wants me to be. He sometimes waits until I've used up all my own strength and I'm desperate and crying out to Him for help. I don't know why I can't just go to

12 Ruth Haley Barton "Strengthening the Soul of Your Leadership." P.28-29

Him first. The "stuff of life" itself sometimes blocks my vision, but He always finds a way to get me back on track.

One morning at 6:00 a.m. I was on my way to the city of Calgary for a "Women in Ministry" conference. I was looking forward to this conference because I had just recently received my credentials as a minister with the Pentecostal Assemblies of Canada. I was looking forward to connecting and networking with other "women in ministry."

I was the last to arrive and as I approached the meeting room, I thought to myself, "What am I actually doing here? I'm not a pastor. I don't even hold a designated "church" position and this is a "women in ministry" conference." I prayed, "God, I'm here and I feel so out of place. I need Your truth to speak to me." For a moment I felt uncomfortable, but God quickly reminded me that He *had* given me a platform for ministry, and I *did* belong here. That calmed my spirit and gave me the peace I needed. I no longer felt out of place.

As the first meeting came to a close, a lady approached me in tears and said, "I know you don't know me, but I felt God wanted me to share this with you." She handed me a piece of paper. I said, "Wow, thank you, I don't know what is on this paper, but I thank you for your obedience in giving it." Later, I opened the paper and I read. *"This chair does not hinder you. I will raise you up and you will fly. I will make your spirit whole and my light will shine through you. My plans for you are great – never doubt."* I was so thankful that God chose this lady to show me He cares about me and to address my earlier concerns.

As a part of our retreat, we all had a little assignment to do. We were all to pray and ask God for a word of encouragement or scripture for someone. Then we were to write it out, put it in a bottle, and place it on a random table in front of someone's seat. Thus, each lady would receive an anonymous note of encouragement. I was excited because I love this openness to the Spirit. I thanked God for this time of refreshment and connection with these ladies. Upon opening my "message in a bottle" I read, *"Stay focused in the pursuit of your testing, and avoid distraction that will take you on a costly detour. Press ahead with all diligence."* My immediate reaction was, "Wow, thank you!" I wanted to give God a high-five!

During the evening service as I was enjoying a beautiful time of worship, God reminded me of the words a man had spoken to me in 2011. He told me, "The Holy Spirit gave me a word for you. He showed me a Lego set. I am putting you back together emotionally, spiritually, and physically. I am building a platform for you to shine. You are not forgotten; you have an anointed part to play. This is a new season for you. Speak the outcomes you want. I will hear. I will answer. I will come in power." Now this time God was showing *me* the Lego blocks, but they formed a completed structure. God impressed on my heart, "Vahen, you are rebuilt. I have put you back together. It is finished and you are whole. Now wait with expectation for your healing. Trust in me."

I cannot tell you how that made me feel, but I just knew that I had to write it down, so I would not question what I felt later. I was also reminded about that man who questioned my father-in-law in Africa about why his son kept this "broken girl." I am so thankful that God does not throw us away in our brokenness. Rather, he rebuilds and restores. In my amazement, I whispered to myself, "God, I could go home right now and I would know that You have blessed me even more than I had asked. Thank you."

During the last session of the conference, the speaker talked about being in alignment with God. I made careful notes of what I heard: "We have everything we need because of Christ's death on the cross: salvation, sanctification, and healing. It is finished. However, you now have to do your part: Believe and receive!"

God was pouring into my heart the confirmation I had asked for. I thought of the verse in Ephesians 3:20 which states, "God can do exceedingly abundantly above all we could ever ask or think." More than ever, I was seeing that maintaining focus on God was very important if I wanted to be strong and have the faith to follow as He leads.

Chapter 17

I'm Listening!

When my friend and I were at Walmart one day waiting in the check-out lane, she asked me a question that set me on a course of discovery. "Vahen, if God were standing here right now and asked you if you want to walk, what would you say?" Immediately I had tears in my eyes. I replied, "I would ask Him if that's what He wanted for me!" Then, that next Sunday morning at church, another good friend of mine said, "Vahen, I feel God wants me to tell you something." She continued, "He wants you to know that He is a gentleman and He does not force Himself on us. He wants to know: 'What do you want?'" With a look of surprise on my face, I explained the conversation I had earlier that week.

God continued to show me that He did not want me to give up. Yes, He was using me in all these different areas because of my disability, but why couldn't I hope for big things from Him? Didn't I believe in what He had promised in Matthew 21:21 "…I say to you, if you have faith and do not doubt, you will not only do what was done to the fig tree, but also if you say to this mountain, 'Be removed and be cast into the sea,' it will be done." How many more times was God going to show me that He wants me to ask big things of Him? He wanted me to have child-like faith to believe in the power He has and, most of all, He wanted me to experience it.

I have special memories of times even as a child of "hearing the Lord" and knowing that He heard me. I recall one such incident. Reflecting on that story builds my faith even today! When we were growing up we often saw my dad working on his boats or working on something in his shed. One of his biggest projects was to build a big fishing boat called the "*Erica Vahen*" (named after my sister and I). We were both really excited about that!

During the time when he had been working night and day on the boat, he had a serious accident. The boat slipped and fell over on him. He was rushed to the hospital where it was determined that he had broken his collarbone. My mom had told me about that story many times, so I asked her to share it.

"Your dad had been in the hospital for one week since the accident and I was going back for my daily visit. When I got to the hospital, he told me he was coming home today. I said "But, you can't go home without the doctor's approval and he's already gone home for the weekend. You'll have to wait until Monday now." Your dad was very determined and I admit I was a little embarrassed because I've never seen him push like this before. The nurses were surprised at his continued insistence as well since he was usually so easy going. The head nurse agreed to contact his doctor at home and the doctor gave your dad permission to leave the hospital for the weekend.

We were just pulling into the driveway at home when you came running out to the car. With unbridled excitement you said to us, "I knew my daddy was coming home today." Surprised, I asked, "How did you know that?" You replied, "Because when you left I went to my room and prayed for him to come home today!" I looked over at your father and then said to you, 'So that's why your dad was acting so strangely at the hospital today. God was answering your prayer.'"

Child-like faith can bring a really major response from God. As I started trusting God to give me that child-like faith again, I felt peace. However, as I continued to work on my book, I couldn't shake the feeling that God wanted me to write about my healing. I thought, "Wasn't it enough for me to just believe and keep it to myself? Now, are You actually nudging me to write about it? I can't write about something that hasn't happened yet, can I?" The very thought of that made me fearful. What will people say about me if I start talking like that? I love my church and the pastors, but will they be open to this way of thinking? Will I be free in my worship or will I go back to my safe place and allow fear to creep back in?

That next morning at church God's presence was so strong in my heart. Our pastor spoke on the healing power of God. Once again, the Lord was pursuing the same conversation with me. As our pastor preached, he asked why can't we see signs and wonders today. If God's power is the same yesterday, today and forever, then we need to step out and have faith to believe. As followers of Christ, can we not believe God's Word and access His healing power? Hearing that message, I knew that God was confirming that He would be with me. He was assuring me that I should not fear, but rather put my trust in where He is leading me.

As Vaughan and I came home from church that morning, I turned to him and said, "Vaughan, I am going to write about my healing because I believe that is what God wants me to do." Then, as clear as anything, I pictured myself standing beside my empty wheelchair looking out into the distance. Although in that moment I had zero evidence in my physical body that a complete healing was even possible, I knew God was showing me that He was going to stretch me farther in my faith. I caught a glimpse of Him not only "completing" the work He had started but also saw that He desired to take me farther in my relationship with Him.

On Tuesday morning my day at work began as it always did. I put my lunch in the fridge and went around to greet my co-workers. That particular morning one of my co-workers said to me, "Vahen, how do you stay so positive and happy all the time? I'm feeling so discouraged because my husband just had open heart surgery and they found cancer. They can't even operate to remove the cancer until his chest heals from his heart surgery. Yet, I look at you and you are so happy despite what you struggle with every day. I feel guilty about being discouraged in my situation."

I hugged her and said, "First of all, don't feel guilty for not being happy right now. Trust me, I have bad days, too. I didn't always have this joy." I had the opportunity to share a little about my life. I told her that even *with* God in your life it is hard to be happy sometimes. I assured her that it's okay for her to be worried and show real human emotion, especially when her husband was so sick.

In that moment I was reminded about what I was doing the night before and I felt I should share with her. I said, "Just last night at my church I was at a special prayer meeting for a man who was dying with cancer. I really feel that this same prayer for healing is for your husband, too." I then proceeded to pray, "God, I believe that You can heal her husband also, so we are asking and believing." She gladly accepted the prayer and thanked me for the encouragement.

I can't remember exactly how much time passed (maybe a few weeks), but I vividly recall the day when that same co-worker approached me. She exclaimed, "I couldn't wait to see you. I have great news! My husband had his next appointment to see how bad the cancer was and to discuss what type of treatment was required. However, after several tests, they told us that the cancer was gone!" We had an emotional embrace and I said, "Praise the Lord!" "Yes," she replied. "Thank you for praying." She then continued to tell me that in the midst of all the planning around her husband's health and the inevitable schedule of treatments, they knew this was going to change their lives. However, never once did they plan for "no cancer." Those words really struck home to my heart. How often have I wanted God to help me, but never expected nor really planned that He will do it? That was a powerful moment for me.

Almost a year later I asked her how her husband was doing. She admitted that although she had been a little nervous when her husband went back for a routine checkup, the results were the same: he was still cancer free! Thank you, God! God wanted me to believe in Him as a God who is not only *able* to heal but also a God that *does* heal.

♡*Chapter 18*

Bumps In The Road

I started working out with a personal trainer in May, 2014, because I knew that if I was going to stay focused and push myself, I needed accountability. I knew that this time I was going to stick with it. I was done with going around in circles. Remembering the word that the Lord had given me, I needed to start doing what I could so God could help me. How many more times could God show me what I had to do before I would listen? I am not suggesting that I could do anything to deserve or earn God's blessing in my life, but I knew He was leading me somewhere and all I had to do was follow. To my surprise, I started seeing noticeable improvements in my overall strength after only one month.

My trainer Nancy wrote me a letter of progress: "Vahen, it is a pleasure to work with you. Even though at times you struggle with pushing through some emotional hurdles, you flourish when given the right encouragement. In the short time we have been working together, your lower extremity muscular strength and endurance continues to increase. Your progress on the spin bike has been truly amazing. You have gone from not being able to do a single rotation without assistance to being able to do 30 seconds on your own within only two weeks. I want to remind you that recovery has its ups and downs. I encourage you to embrace both. This is all a part of the recovery process. I also want to commend you on your work ethic. You always bring 110% to each session."

As a result of this increased muscle strength, I started seeing improvements in my overall health and digestion. In my life, this is a huge blessing! I told my husband that I was going to the bathroom more often and with better success. All I needed now was to shorten the time spent completing the task and to do it without medication.

As I started my physiotherapy again, I was now literally living in what the Lord had said to me after I recommitted my life to God. The word that He had impressed upon my heart was that I was to do what I could and He would do the rest. He did exactly what He said He would do and I saw and felt the difference. People say seeing is believing, but that was not always the case with me. Previously even when I was seeing results, I constantly grew weary and gave up. But since I've been writing my book, I knew I needed to keep pushing forward. That's when Nancy came into my life. I was convinced that God placed her in my life to ensure I wouldn't give up. Even on the days when I would tell her that I wasn't up to working out because I was struggling either emotionally or physically, she would say that she would come anyway. Our sessions began with her faithfully encouraging me to do what I could. Somehow she would always get me to do more than I thought I could do. This discovery was always such an encouragement to me.

Only four months after I started working out with Nancy, I was in a car accident. It was severe enough that my car was written off. I was merging onto the highway on my way to meet a friend for dinner. At that point another driver coming toward me ran a red light. I was able to brake and stop in time to avoid him. However, the driver in the vehicle behind me didn't have time to stop. He rear-ended me with his big service truck. He immediately jumped out of his truck and rushed to see if I was okay. At first I thought I was; but, as soon as I saw the bumper of my car in my back seat, the tears began to roll down my face. We both pulled our vehicles into the nearest parking lot and he rushed over and offered to help me out of my car. At the same moment, we were both drawn to look down at the red nail polish stain on my tan leather seats. I had been meaning to remove that, but with a look of shock on his face he said, "Are you bleeding?" I kind of chuckled a bit and said, "No, that's just nail polish." In disbelief, he reached out and felt the stain just to make sure that indeed it was an old nail polish stain. I think he must have thought I was in shock and I didn't really know if I was bleeding or not.

Thankfully, no one was seriously injured but my car was totalled and now I was stranded. Vaughan was working out of town, so I called some really close friends of mine to pick me up from the accident. I contacted Vaughan to let him know what had happened. I assured him I was okay and that I was being taken care of. I really looked forward to seeing him in a couple of days upon his return. Since I was now without a vehicle I used a taxi to get around when needed. My back and neck muscles took a beating and I knew I would have some extreme back pain to work through. I informed my employer about the accident and wisely requested some time off to recover.

Surprisingly, after only a couple of weeks, I was back to work with only minimal pain. However, during the time spent being on my back and not working out, I lost some of the muscle mass that I had built up. The accident set me behind about two to three months in my progress. I became discouraged and even a little depressed. I knew I had much to be thankful for. It could have been much worse, but this interruption made me feel like I was starting over AGAIN! It felt too much like the old patterns of stopping and losing ground. For the next four months, Nancy was able to help me overcome some intense emotional and physical pain. She said to me, "Vahen, these past few months have been a testament that recovery has its ups and downs. However, you have demonstrated not only what it means to have strength and determination, but that you can have joy through your circumstances. You continue to progress and achieve each goal we set. The sky's the limit for you."

I knew I couldn't quit, but I knew this would be one of the biggest struggles of my recovery that I would have to work through. The discouragement of this accident was making everything (especially my bathroom time) seem ten times worse. On one occasion it was around 2:00 a.m. and I was still sitting in the bathroom. Through my pain I cried out, "God! I don't want to read my Bible! I don't want to look for words on a page! I want *You* to speak to me! I want *You* to tell me why you have not taken this pain! Why have You not healed me?" When I was done yelling, I just sat there crying. Finally, I said, "Okay God, I'm done yelling and I'm ready to listen."

Through my tears, the Lord began to show me a field. In the vision I could see Him standing in that field. As I watched Him, there was a fog rising all around me and I was finding it hard to see Him. However, I knew He could still see me. Then the words, "I can't see perfectly" came into my mind. Immediately I thought, "There is a verse in the Bible about that." So I googled the words "I can't see perfectly." What I found was "Now we see things imperfectly, like puzzling reflections in a mirror, but then we will see everything with perfect clarity. All that I know now is partial and incomplete, but then I will know everything completely, just as God now knows me completely." I Corinthians 13:12 (NLT) Those four simple words that He showed me in that vision were so meaningful and encouraging. The "fog" of my frustration gave me only limited understanding of what I was experiencing. However, He had complete, unobstructed view. He was telling me that I could trust His all-knowing and all-caring love for me.

With everything I was going through, there were times that I thought I would actually break. I remember well one day that I pulled into my garage, parked the car, and just sat there crying. In my utter frustration and discouragement, I began thinking how easy it would be if I could just fall asleep here in my garage with the engine running. The enemy was trying to convince me that I could just fall asleep and wake up with Jesus. Even though I knew that was a lie, I didn't want to fight any more. I was just emotionally and physically spent. I knew that if didn't get relief from my pain, I would have a complete breakdown. I realized I was hurting, but didn't know what to do. I didn't really want to end my life, but I longed to come to an end of all my pain and setbacks. I didn't know how many more times I could keep picking myself up and pushing to keep moving forward.

That next day my aunt and I had tentative plans for her to come and visit me. I was really looking forward to seeing her. Her schedule changed and she called and asked if we could reschedule. After I hung up the phone I just broke down and cried. I knew that if my aunt were aware of how much I needed her right now, she would certainly be here. I didn't want to go back to being that person who pretends everything is okay in order to appear strong; so, I swallowed my pride and called her back. Through my tears I told her how much I needed her. Then, in less than two seconds she said, "I'm on my way." I really needed to feel that love and support. It was a huge blessing to have her there for me. (I know I have thanked her many times, but I feel it won't be until she reads this that she will truly understand how precious she is to me).

I found that risking vulnerability with others and with God often means letting them know how I'm really feeling without fear of rejection. Even though I knew my aunt would never reject me, I was learning that it was okay to ask for help. It meant a lot to be able to lean on close friends and God during those difficult times.

During this recovery time, the insurance company was paying for my physio treatments three times a week to assist with the pain and muscle tightness caused from the accident. One day when I was laying on the bed receiving my treatment, I could hear a lady talking to her physiotherapist.

This lady had also been in a car accident and I could hear her moaning in pain. I overheard her therapist telling her she needed to rest and not lift anything heavy. We were only separated by a thin curtain between our beds. This conversation I overheard just broke my heart. Apparently, she faced moving out of her home at the end of the month. It was only 10 days away and she was still trying to pack. Her husband was working a lot of overtime and he was also struggling with his health. On top of that, they were new to Canada and didn't know many people to ask for help. She also had four little children to take care of and she could barely move without pain.

As I heard the desperation in her voice, my heart ached. I lay there with my heating pack and was moved to tears. I knew that I needed to get her contact information and at least try to help. I was no better off in my situation, but I knew I had to try. I introduced myself and told her I had overheard her conversation. When I asked if I could have her number, she said, "But you don't know me. Why would you want to help?" I just replied, "I know what it's like to be in need and to have people come alongside you when you feel you are alone."

Later the next day she shared her life story with me. She told me how she has had so many things taken from her. One major loss was the death of her 4-year-old son several years before. She said that it was just too much to bear. It made her question her faith in a loving God. She said, 'I was really beginning to think that God had forgotten me and my family and that no one cared, but then you came along."

We talked for a while and I let her know that I was going to be contacting my church, Evangel, to see if they could help with her situation. I asked her if that was okay. She went quiet for a moment and I could hear her start to cry. She asked, "You're from Evangel?" I replied, "Yes, is that a problem?" She then told me that she had been referred to Evangel by someone else the same day we met. However, she felt so discouraged and decided not to call. I was amazed at how God works things out. This whole "chance meeting" was a clear indication to her that God had not forgotten her. I realized that if I had not been in that accident, I probably would never have met her. I was just glad that I was in the right place at the right time to offer this help. This whole incident built my faith, too.

I requested help from my church and within the next few days some ladies from our church came to her home and helped pack up her belongings. One lady and her family even brought clothes and school supplies for all the kids. You can only imagine how that was received. One of the pastors at my church also sent an email to the men's group to see if they could help with the move at the end of the month. I was amazed yet again how everyone came together to help this family in time of great need. She was so overwhelmed with gratitude. She told me she believed that I was an angel God sent to help her and her family. She said "It's because you cared enough to help that I am learning to trust in God again."

A few short weeks after we met, she started attending my small group book study and then she accepted Jesus into her heart. Soon her whole family began attending our church. The Lord certainly had a big plan in mind that day when I overheard her tears through that thin divider curtain at my physiotherapy appointment. What an illustration that His ears are always open to our cry. I marvel at His ways!

I had a friend tell me about services being held in a nearby church. She said that God was speaking into people's lives and some were even receiving healing. I thought, "That's exactly where I need to be." After the last few months of feeling emotionally, physically and spiritually drained, I felt I could sure use a time of refreshing. So a couple of my close friends and I went with the hope that we too would receive something special from God.

We were standing around talking after the service when a gentleman came to me and said; "This may sound really odd and I don't know what this will mean to you, but I just have to tell you what God showed me when you were worshiping earlier." He said, "God showed me by the Spirit that you had wings on your back. They were big wings that spanned out wide on either side of you."

I began to weep and replied, "You have no idea what those words mean to me. I have to share with you something that my mother told me a few months ago." I then proceeded to tell him that when my mother was visiting with the pastor's wife from the church where I grew up, they were talking about when I was first diagnosed with Transverse Myelitis. This lady told my mother that when she first heard I was sick she felt God say to her, "Vahen's wings may be clipped now, but she will fly again."

God's timing is truly amazing! I told the gentleman about recently being in a car accident which had affected my recovery progress. "If there were ever a time when I felt like my wings were clipped, it would be now. For God to show you that He has restored my wings was just the encouragement I needed. Thank you."

God was reassuring me that He was still with me. That gave me great comfort. While it is possible that not everyone accepts the prophetic realm, it is a reality that the Lord longs to communicate His heart to us. Even if an incident like this one may seem like fantasy to some, the Lord was using those words from a stranger to assure me that He knows every intimate detail of my life and loves me unconditionally. That gave me great confidence. Only a God who is real could engineer a moment like that in order to confirm my trust in Him

There is no question about the Lord's faithfulness and His creativity to continually communicate to me during the entire period of that frustrating setback. There were so many "bumps in the road" during that time; perhaps they were even mountains to be moved. I would rather have had weeks of a perfectly straight, problem-free path. Instead, the Lord used several different people in such a variety of settings to confirm His love. The encouragement from His communication to me kept me from quitting. I discovered that I could push through and find a strength from Him that I had not previously known. He was breaking the old patterns of going around in circles. Now I was gaining momentum to be going farther than I had ever known.

♡Chapter 19

It's Happening

A friend of mine who leads a Bible Study on Monday nights at our church was beginning the "Breaking Free" series by Beth Moore. She asked me if I would bring the anointing oil and pray with any ladies who wanted prayer after the meeting. I felt in my heart that I was meant to be there and gladly accepted her invitation.

We both felt that we should meet ahead of time and pray about the evening. During our prayer time together God showed me people coming for prayer. And, He was standing right in front of me. As each person came for prayer we could see where they needed healing. Some had broken hearts and others needed healing of the mind. As they came, God was putting them back together one by one and they were going away healed.

When I turned to my friend and told her what I had just seen, she had a look of shock on her face. She said, "Vahen, when I first did this series it was at a very low point in my life. God showed me that He was healing my heart and that He was putting me back together." There was no question in our minds that God had something very special for this group and that people would truly be "set free."

I approached that first night asking God to give me strength and wisdom. As I prayed over each lady I felt something happening in my own heart. I felt God saying that these prayers of healing were for me, too. I actually even felt that a healing was happening in my own body. Yes, for a long while I knew God had been speaking to me about my healing. I was trusting Him even though I didn't see any proof. But, this time was different. Something *was* changing.

Up until that opening night of the Bible Study I had been making some progress with my recovery. Yet, one area of continued struggle was with my digestive system. Following that prayer time as the Lord was working in the lives of the ladies, something was definitely happening inside of my own body. After I came home that night, I had one of the best bathroom visits to date. In my world that meant going in less than two hours. This time it was indeed less than two hours and without medication. I was encouraged but yet still doubted. Success for just one time was not enough to make me believe I was now healed after having battled in this area for sixteen years.

The very next day I saw a pressure sore starting and I was in a lot of pain and discomfort. It was a very scary day for me because I had never had a pressure sore before. I was always so careful. A pressure sore occurs when a person is sitting or lying in one position for a long period of time. In order for it to heal, you have to avoid putting any pressure on that spot for up to a week or longer. The enemy was trying to discourage me by making me think, "Yeah right, your body is not healing. It's getting worse. Just look at the pain you're in." Fear and doubt were trying to creep back in, but I began to pray and I also asked my close friends to pray.

The next morning the pressure sore was gone and I felt only a little discomfort. I can't describe the relief I felt. I was so thankful. And, I was even more convinced that God was healing me. I made a fresh resolve to ignore the lies of the enemy that were causing me to doubt or fear. Rather, I would look forward with great expectation to what God would do in my life.

I can hardly believe how this new confidence in God changed me. My thinking became: "Hey, the Bible works!" This was a profound revelation for someone who's been reading the Bible her whole life. Now, however I was reading with much more consistency. A deep-rooted foundation was developing and I realized I was not so quick to give into fear. Instead I had more courage to express what God was doing in my life. God was giving me the power to pray against my fears and the boldness to step out and obey His leadings. I wanted to go farther in my walk with God, and, because I no longer settled for what I had before, He was giving me much more.

Near the end of January 2015, only four months away from our annual ladies' retreat, I was reminded about what God had laid on my heart at the previous year's retreat. I had written in my journal that God was going to give me a testimony of my healing. I would grow in overcoming fear. I would have increased trust in where He was leading me. I was convinced that this was going to happen. Now, with the retreat only four months away, I couldn't help but think, "What if I was wrong? Maybe God didn't really tell me that. Maybe it was just me. Immediately I said out loud, "I am writing about the healing power of God and believing that He is healing me right now. I know God is in control, so I *do* have a testimony!"

Before the first week of February had ended, I started to experience some major changes in my digestion and bathroom routine. I knew it was a good thing, but with these improvements came some new challenges. I found it difficult to control exactly when I would have to use the bathroom. This was very stressful while trying to balance my part-time job. My husband suggested that I should see my doctor about taking a medical leave from work so that I could focus on my health. This was a tough decision to make, but ultimately I felt like this was the best choice.

In the months prior to my medical leave, I had consulted a specialist. He suggested that I track my bathroom routine to see if we could determine the cause or factors that might be affecting me. This was an odd thing for me to journal about, but I began to do so. At the point of my medical leave I had been keeping a diary for about a month or so. To my surprise, I started seeing unbelievable improvements in my health only days after leaving work. I couldn't ignore this pattern because I was recording everything. I left work on the fifth of February and on the sixth I wrote in my diary: "no medication." Then on the seventh: "no medication" was again the journal entry. After about two weeks of documenting the results which were happening without medication, I actually believed that something miraculous was happening in my body.

While doing my exercises one day, I felt God say to me, "Vahen, I am healing you and you are not even believing it. I want you to believe." He reminded me of Hebrews 11:1 "Now faith is the substance of things hoped for, the evidence of things not seen." God was wanting me to believe in what I was seeing. This was life-changing for me. I was writing the results out, but I was still in disbelief. I was trying to dismiss or explain it away, but the results were undeniable. God was healing me from the inside out. I said, "God, I am ready for more." After sixteen years of the bathroom routine controlling my life and not being able to go without medication, I can now say that God is healing me and I am medication free!

After I finally accepted that God was healing me, I did not hesitate to share this exciting news with the ladies of the retreat leadership team. They were equally excited about the news and asked me to share this testimony at our annual ladies' retreat. I was able to share what God was doing and to encourage the ladies not to doubt what God plants in their hearts. We draw strength from the Word of the Lord found in 2 Corinthians 1:20. "For all the promises of God in Him *are* Yes, and in Him Amen, to the glory of God through us." God is making each step clear and, because I am trusting in God and have faith in the evidence of things not yet seen, *it's happening!*

Chapter 20

Sustaining Power

It is hard for me to comprehend at times, but the way that the events of my life have unfolded is so accurately described in Romans 8:28. "And we know that all things work together for good to those who love God, to those who are the called according to *His* purpose." His plans are definitely different than any I would have chosen; but, the way He has put my life together proves that it was for my good. He not only took all the things in my life and turned them around for good, but He was showing me that He can take me farther than I had ever imagined. My confidence increased as I allowed Him full control and trusted in Him.

Yes, God was drawing me to believe for a miracle in my life. However, I was beginning to realize that the miracle of healing was not even the greatest of goals. The Lord was showing me that my total dependency on Him is the greatest privilege and focus of my life. Even though I loved and served God all my life, why did I find it so hard to relinquish full control? I needed to focus more on a genuine relationship with God rather than working to *achieve* something from God.

After I re-committed my life to God, my friend and I were both invited to speak at my parents' church in Newfoundland. I felt so weak and unworthy. For myself, I knew I needed God to give me the strength and wisdom to speak what He wanted me to share. So for the three months before my trip, my friend and I devoted more time in prayer and reading the Bible. We also connected regularly to pray together. For me, I decided that less time in front of the TV was also what I needed to keep my heart and mind focused on only the things that He wanted to say. As a result, I feel God really blessed our time there.

However, I didn't understand why I was feeling emotionally and physically drained when I returned from the trip. Previously it had taken me weeks to recover from my trip to Africa. Even though it was mostly my physical body that was affected, yet that ministry trip abroad had also left me feeling emotionally and spiritually drained. This trip home to Newfoundland was no different. I didn't think I was strong enough to continue this type of ministry. It was during that time that God showed me I needed to build up my endurance for the ministry He was leading me into. I needed to grow my spiritual muscles. Although these short-term fasts were great, they were not enough to build any kind of endurance for spiritual strength.

About that time, I received an email from my father-in-law explaining that reading the Bible through each time in a different way or in a different version can sometimes provide a better understanding of scripture. For example, reading it chronologically would give you one perspective and reading it topically gives you another perspective and so on. I laughed and thought to myself, "Each time? Try *one* time!" I was strongly convicted. How many times have I started but failed to follow through? Too many times to count, I'm afraid. I realized that drawing closer to the Lord was just like building any other relationship. It takes time and commitment to get to know the person. My heart was in the right place, but I never seemed to make the commitment to go farther in my relationship with

God. I was convinced that because I wanted it so much, God would simply see my desire and just give it to me. How did I think I could grow spiritually and not put out the effort and commitment it required? Don't get me wrong, I did my daily devotions and even read my Bible and prayed, but there was no depth. Yet I continued to have this longing to go deeper with God. I felt a lot of my prayers were just me telling God all the things I needed or wanted. I hadn't learned to just sit and listen or wait to hear what He had to say.

In January, 2014, we had a special speaker at our church who talked about the power of prayer and knowing the Word of God. The first night during prayer time, he prayed over me and said that God was calling me into a deeper relationship with Him. And, He was calling me to be a woman of prayer. That was nothing new to me, but this time those words just resounded within my heart. I knew it was time to step out and really commit to going farther in my walk with God. Then, later that week we were also given a challenge to read the Bible through in one year. I knew that I was going to commit *this* time, because this was definitely a key to my deeper relationship with God.

Now fast forward to the end of 2014: My initial thought as I approached my year-end goal of reading the Bible through was, "Yay! I did it! Now I can return to my previous routine of daily devotions." But instantly, I had a slight feeling of panic and thought, "No! That was my spiritual food this past year." I had proven God to be true to His Word. Yes, I could look back and see how reading God's Word - even when I didn't feel like it - was developing discipline in my life. I was growing my spiritual muscles. I was getting to know the Author on a deeper level. I was learning to wait on God and listen. I realized that I had developed that deeper relationship with God as a result of reading the Bible every day and taking time to talk with Him in prayer. I could not believe it had taken me so long to really "get it."

So my decision was obvious; I kept the routine of reading my Bible through into the next year as well. Was it easy? No. At times it felt like I was reading words on a page that had no meaning. But as I spent time each day with God, He was drawing me closer, and I came to crave that time with Him. I was truly developing spiritual discipline in my life.

I often think about Olympic athletes when they are in training. How many times do they look at their routines and exercises and wonder if it's too hard? At times, it likely feels redundant or pointless. Then, once they get to participate in the Olympics, they look back and see how all their hard work and perseverance was worth it.

My perspective of reading the Bible and spending time with God had changed tremendously. It became more than just a "goal to accomplish "or a "task to complete." It became my strength. And, I understood more than ever that the joy of the Lord is my strength. My passion to share this with others was confirmed: "Don't forget your spiritual food. Without it you will not have the strength to fight and overcome the challenges you face."

Out of my commitment to be disciplined in reading the Word of God, I developed the spiritual strength I needed. The consistent time with the Lord and His Word confirmed that my total dependency on Him truly is the greatest privilege and focus of my life. If you could listen in to some of my heart-talk with the Lord you would hear: "How could I come close to you God and *not* believe? I see Your awesome power. I see that You have the power to bless me. You desire to bless me more than I could ever ask or think. I now have increased confidence in Your words from Jeremiah 29:11. "For I know the plans I have for you," declares the Lord, "plans to prosper you and not to harm you, plans to give you hope and a future." (NIV)

♡ *Chapter 21*

Faithful to Complete It!

My whole life I have desired to have a relationship with God that is not only life-changing, but would have world-changing potential. God has shown me that to have that world-changing faith I would sometimes have to believe for the things not yet seen. That has been both a valuable principle and an ongoing learning experience. Reaching those things "not yet seen" also requires perseverance.

These lessons about perseverance in spiritual progress have been often illustrated as I've pushed forward in my physical strength-building goals. My trainer Nancy continued to be amazed at my progress. She said, "It's been just over a year since we've begun this journey together, and you continue to progress and achieve any goals we set for you. For example, you set the goal to walk to the end of your block with your walker, by the end of June 2015; you accomplished it by June 26, 2015. You can now cycle upwards of six minutes independently and last three minutes on the treadmill at a speed of 0.9mph. You continue to progress past each assistive device we use. You are now at the point of transitioning into unassisted steps. Continue to plunge forward with the confidence that God has given you. You can overcome any obstacle thrown in your way, because He has begun a work in you that He will complete."

About a week before I made my first unassisted steps, I stood to my feet and tried to make a step. I thought, "How in the world am I going to walk without the walker if I feel my feet are glued to the floor?" It seemed nearly impossible. Then, the night before I made my first unassisted steps, I was talking to God, "Lord, if I am going in the direction that You want me to go and I'm not just believing in this because *I* want it, then please show me more progress." I woke up that morning and I *knew* something was different and I had to try. And if you could have seen my video, you would have seen the excitement of reaching that milestone of my *first unassisted step!*

Pressing forward to discover that the Lord really is able to complete a work in and through me has been a challenge, but oh, so rewarding. One vital lesson I have learned as I've grown in perseverance is to keep pushing despite what I am feeling. It's easy to think that this whole concept of learning how to persevere in spite of what you're feeling should get less difficult as you move forward. I have found instead that it actually gets more intense. The only difference is that I have learned to stop fighting the battles in my own strength and give up control to God sooner.

The months surrounding the completion of this book were some of the most challenging, yet the most amazing, months of my life. I knew I would face some internal struggles as I prepared to share my story with the world, but I really didn't fully understand to what extent. One of my editors said to me, "The enemy doesn't want you to get this book out there, Vahen, and he is making every effort to derail it."

A frequent tool of the enemy is to attempt to distract you from God's purpose in your life. If he can't distract you through personal failings or sin in your life, then he will use outside influences and relationships to try and take your focus off God.

This quote from Allen Randolph was very helpful to me. "A distraction can be a brief, pleasant distraction. However, any diversion has the potential for a misdirection you may not intend. Distractions can come in many forms—ambivalence, fear, doubts, busyness, tiredness, delays, disappointments, opposition, others' opinions, mistreatment, competing opinions and/or people's expectations. That can be costly if not noticed and corrected. Every step in a wrong direction diminishes accomplishing your purpose and faithfulness to your calling[13]."

During a recent time of dealing with my own distractions, I remember crying out to God in my bedroom. I was dealing with an agonizing conflict with another individual and I was so tempted to use my own words and react in my own strength. Instead, I felt I needed to give this to God and trust Him to take care of it as I knew this was much bigger than me. I said "God, I don't understand. Please give me Your strength and Your wisdom." In that intense pain, I was reminded of that moment as a teenager when I first got the call to go into ministry and I sang that song entitled "I'd Rather Have Jesus" by Rhea Miller. One of those lines came back to me: "I'd rather have Jesus than man's applause, I'd rather be faithful to His dear cause[14]." I praised God that I had Him on my side. The other intense emotion I was feeling was Vaughan's love and support. The support that was lacking early in our marriage was now undeniably strong and real. We prayed together every day for peace and protection. I felt I truly understood what it meant to forsake my own understanding and choose to follow God's leading. It is more important to me to do God's will and have

13 Allen Randolph; "Everyday Life";
    http://www.allenrandolph.com/?tag=philippians-313-14
14 "I'd rather have Jesus than Silver or Gold." Hymn Writer: Rhea Miller,
    Music written by: George Beverly Shea; "Hymn History";
    http://hishymnhistory.blogspot.ca/2012/11/id-rather-have-jesus.html

the love and support of my husband than to strive for approval.

Distractions may come from events in life that we can't necessarily control, such as health issues, work stress, or even unexpected financial costs. Vaughan and I have learned how to persevere together and grow in our relationship with each other and with God despite any distraction or obstacle that comes our way. Distractions really do come in all forms. It's not always because someone is intentionally causing you pain. No, it's sometimes from people with the best of intentions. People have made me question my faith, my dreams, or God's plan for me, because of their "best intentioned" actions or words.

A prime negative example was when I was first in the hospital with Transverse Myelitis. I was told that maybe the reason why God hasn't healed me was because I had sin in my life or I perhaps didn't have enough faith. I've found it very valuable to surround myself with people I can trust and respect. Friends and mentors who are spiritually anchored in the Word of God or who can provide empowering, positive support bring such value and actually promote God's purposes in and through me. I'm learning the principle of being mindful of who you allow to speak into your life, no matter how well you know someone. You can accept their words, but always take these words before God and allow Him to validate them through His Word.

Stepping out to do God's work comes with a price. I was confronted with the reality that if I planned to persevere and go farther in my walk with Christ, I would need to reach a deeper level of personal surrender and give Him more room in my life. That meant not only letting some relationships go, but even changing how I would spend my time and money. This was a real struggle for me. It did not always "feel good," but God was teaching me to surrender my will and my understanding to Him. He was showing me that if I didn't lean on my own understanding but choose instead to acknowledge Him, He would direct my paths. (Proverbs 3:5) He wanted me to trust that He would take care of everything in my life, even my mistakes, as I yielded to Him.

Perseverance meant pushing past uncertainty to seek the will of God and step out in ministry. This has resulted in taking the biggest step of faith yet in my walk with God. In this "forward thrust," it would make sense that I would face some of my biggest emotional and spiritual battles.

Looking back on everything that I have been through in my life, I want to thank God for leading me through my pain into a deeper relationship with Him and for taking me farther than I ever thought possible. God definitely took my pain and turned it into a "door of hope." This new mindset gives me a whole new appreciation for James 1:1-4, "My brethren, count it all joy when you fall into various trials, knowing that the testing of your faith produces patience. But let patience have *its* perfect work, that you may be perfect and complete, lacking nothing."

In the days of my wanderings, I had tried everything and still didn't know where to turn until I decided to give God another chance. It wasn't a church or a religion but rather my genuine relationship with God that made all the difference. From my own progress and discovery, I know I can now share with authority that no matter how tough my circumstances are, God will always be enough to help me overcome! I now look everyday with eager expectation for when my healing will be complete. I trust in God and the truth of this verse: "...being confident of this very thing, that He who has begun a good work in you will complete it...." Philippians 1:6 (NIV)

♡Chapter 22

But Wait, There's More!

There's a game Vaughan bought recently called, "But Wait, There's More!" The object of the game is to give your best sales pitch to win the votes of the other players. A product card is drawn for each round. Then each player is given three "feature" cards and you choose the one you feel would best sell that product to the other players. You are given 30 seconds to pitch your product using your unique feature card. But, after 15 seconds you have to stop and say, "But wait, there's more!" Then you draw another random feature card from the deck and promote the new, additional feature into your product pitch.

Don't you feel that life is like that sometimes? You start off having a plan; but, halfway through, life throws in a "But Wait, There's More!" and you have to somehow fit this new twist into your plan. You just get to the point where you've learned to cope with the situation and then, out of the blue, something else happens! Your first thought is, "Really? But, I can't handle any more!" I know that has often been the case in my life. However, do we ever consider that God wants to bless us *more*? I wonder if as we struggle in our circumstances, we could turn our view around and realize that God is perhaps trying to say to us, "Just wait; there's more!" And, that "more" doesn't just mean more challenge but actually more blessing from our trustworthy Lord.

We are reminded in Ephesians 3:20 that our God is able to do exceedingly abundantly above all that we ask or think. I believe this verse is God's way of saying "But wait, there's more." Yet, often we continue to settle for what we can see, hear, taste, touch, or feel, and we don't believe for more.

It's been a challenge to write a book where the story is not complete, but God keeps doing more than I could have asked for. I am amazed at how God could allow me to walk a life of freedom, no longer a slave to my sins. I am unworthy yet I feel free and forgiven, and I carry no shame or guilt. Not only that, but after sixteen years, who would have thought it possible to take independent steps and anticipate the day when I can leave this chair behind? However, here I am living in freedom with great expectation. Many times in this journey, I've yelled at God and doubted. But now I say, "Thank you, God, for giving me exceedingly abundantly more than I could ever ask or think." He keeps bringing me farther than I ever thought possible. I have learned that if you are never tested you will never know what you're capable of. And, if you don't learn to trust in God, you can never know what He's capable of.

I wanted to give up after Bible College, but God said, "Vahen, just wait—there's more." I wanted to get an instant healing, but God said, "Vahen, just wait—there's more." I wanted to leave my marriage because I had lost all hope, but God said, "Vahen, just wait—there's more." I wanted to give up on my exercise and quit, but God said, "Vahen, just wait—there's more."

Vaughan and I have often told God that we knew what was best. But we are now learning to say, "God, we'll wait, because we know there's more." We invite you to join us in that confidence and receive a spirit of adventure to discover God's intended "more" for *your* life. One thing is sure: We are *GOING FARTHER!*

 One More Step

I don't want to wait on the sidelines.
I don't want to waste my time.
Looking back, wishing that, I'd done it differently.
Why do I carry burdens that aren't mine?
Walk around pretending I'm fine.
And in vain, I hold the chains, that no one else can see.
Always thinking I can earn your love but I can't, no I can't.
And yet there's nothing I could do that will make it go.

So I put one foot in front of the other.
Keep walking, keep walking.
Each day a little bit farther.
Just keep walking, keep walking.
One more step, don't turn back around.

Kelly Marie Elford
Download her song for free at: https://soundcloud.com/kellyelford
kellyelfordmusic@outlook.com
All songs written and performed by Kelly Elford ©

♡*Acknowledgments*

"And when can I read your book?" Those seven words planted seeds into my heart that grew to enable me to present to you – My Book! God was growing dreams in me I didn't even know I had and showing me He wants to give me *more*! So many people have encouraged me and believed in me throughout this process. That encouragement plus their patient persistence have carried me farther as a writer than I ever thought possible.

My family definitely has believed in me and at times "believed *for* me." Thank you to each one of our families. Father John, you are so much more than an observing father-in-law. You are a spiritual mentor and sometimes the conduit used by God to push me outside my comfortable box. Mom, you are my biggest cheerleader. You tell me that your dream is to now help your children fulfill *their* dreams. What more could a daughter ask for? No one will know the countless hours we have spent laughing, crying, and praying together.

At the early stages of considering the book Mary-lynne Middelkoop became key to sorting through many, many thoughts and ideas. Mary-lynne, thank you for helping me get to that next phase as I overcame some personal hurdles en route.

The next major step was to send an email to Peggy Kennedy. I knew her as a speaker and minister; and, she had now also authored several books. Her response to that first email led to our relationship as my editor, coach, and spiritual mentor. Thank you, Peggy, for assuring me that the "Master Author" would bring ideas, images, high points, and even phrases to me. She has made this process about more than just words on a page, but about enriching and empowering encouragement. I thank the Lord for bringing Peggy into my life for such a time as this to share my passion and push my book forward to completion.

I have been amazed at the times of "breakthrough" as the writing progressed. I thank the Lord for these reminders that He really was the one who called me to this assignment. I also am aware that breakthroughs would not have come without the earnest commitment of the intercessory team. Thank you for your strategic intercession at each phase of this journey. Your prayers have protected the process and will continue to guard His purposes.

I am so thrilled to say that my vision for my book cover was captured perfectly, and it's all thanks to Rick and my delightful team of "assistants" who creatively partnered to visualize joy along the pathway of perseverance.

And to my loving husband Vaughan: my heart is overflowing as I recall our journey. Together we have faced mountains and giants, yet we have come through to the other side standing stronger than ever. Vaughan, thank you for keeping me grounded but still letting me fly! Thank you for constantly supporting this call to write "our story." There's no greater joy than being partners together and partners with our wonderful Lord.

And, most of all I want to thank my Lord who truly is "...able to do exceedingly abundantly above all that we ask or think, according to the power that works in us." (Ephesians 3:20) It is because of Him, that I can declare — I am *GOING FARTHER!*

♡ *About the Author*

Vahen King is a graduate of Theological Studies from Masters College & Seminary, a credentialed Licensed Minister with the PAOC, and a Life Purpose Coach. Vahen acknowledges that God is number one in her life and owes all her success and happiness to Him. She believes that all the events in her life–both good and bad, have given her a unique platform to show God's glory and unfailing love.

Vahen currently lives with her husband Vaughan in Alberta, Canada, where they are involved in their local church and community. Vahen states, that she has devoted her life to sharing her journey with others in the hope that people will be challenged and inspired to *go farther*!

Stay Connected

Vahen would like to invite you to stay connected with her and be a part of her journey as she ministers to the world around her.

Visit www.vahenking.com to:

- Contact Vahen regarding any speaking engagement, motivational seminar, or inquire about Life Coaching
- Join Vahen's newsletter to be included in any praise reports, prayer requests, tour dates, or new publications
- View more photos, or follow her on different social media streams
- Receive online benefits like coupons and special book offers that you can use and share with your friends

Share Your Thoughts

Please share with us if you were inspired or encouraged by Vahen's story at *goingfarther@vahenking.com*

CPSIA information can be obtained at www.ICGtesting.com
Printed in the USA
LVOW11s0811120816

499645LV00001B/2/P